"Discover the limitless potential of computer science and engineering with this accessible and comprehensive guide, tailored specifically for non-CSE Enthusiasts looking to gain a deeper understanding of the intricate world of technology."

INTRODUCTION TO MATHEMATICS FOR COMPUTING (ALGORITHMS AND DATA STRUCTURES)

Computer Science Engineering (CSE) For Non-CSE Enthusiasts

Enamul Haque

Copyright © 2023 by Enamul Haque

All rights reserved. Except for brief excerpts in a book review or scholarly publication, no reproduction or use of this book or any portion thereof is permitted without the publisher's prior written consent.

Last update: April 2023

ISBN: 9781447771302
Imprint: lulu.com

Publisher:
ENEL PUBLICATIONS
London, United Kingdom
Cover Photo by Ricardo Lima[i]

- THE STORY BEHIND THIS BOOK -

Once upon a time, a curious student had always been interested in mathematics and its application in computing but had never explored the subject in depth. They were intimidated by the technical jargon and complex concepts surrounding mathematics for computing, but they wanted to learn more.

That's when they stumbled upon a book that promised to demystify the world of mathematics for computing for non-technical enthusiasts. The book provides a comprehensive overview of everything one needs to know about algorithms and data structures in a language anyone can understand.

Excited by the prospect of finally understanding the mysteries of mathematics for computing, the student bought the book and started reading. As they delved deeper into the pages, they discovered a treasure trove of information about mathematical foundations, sets, relations, logic, probability, optimization, and more.

They learned about the basic concepts and principles of mathematical structures in computing and how to apply them to algorithms and data structures. They discovered how to solve complex problems and optimize solutions using mathematical techniques. They even learned about the applications of mathematics in various fields like cryptography, image processing, and machine learning.

With every page turn, the student felt more empowered and excited about their newfound knowledge. They felt like they were finally part of the world of mathematics for computing and couldn't wait to explore it further.

If you are a non-technical student who is always curious about mathematics for computing, then this book is the perfect guide to help you discover the wonders of this exciting field. With its easy-to-understand language and comprehensive coverage of all the essential topics, this book will transform you from a curious outsider to a confident insider in no time.

So why wait? Get your copy today and start exploring the exciting world of mathematics for computing!

ENEL PUBLICATIONS
London, United Kingdom
Revision 01 – July 2024

CONTENTS

Introduction 1
   Who is this book for? 3
      What will you learn in this book? 3

CHAPTER 1 5

Introduction To Mathematics For Computing 7
   Definitions 8
   Mathematical Foundations 9
   Basic Mathematical Concepts for Computing 11

Foundations of Mathematical Structures in Computing 13
   Sets 13
   Set Operations 14
   Subsets and power sets 14
   Cartesian product of sets 15
   Sequences and Series 15
   Definition of sequences 16
   Arithmetic and geometric sequences 17
   Series and convergence 18
   Functions 18
   Function notation and domain and range 19
   Types of functions: injective, surjective, and bijective 20
   Composition of functions 21
   Inverse functions 22
   Binary Relations 22
   Properties of relations 24
   Equivalence relations and partitions 25
   Partial order relations 26

Logical Foundations of Mathematics for Computing 27
   Propositions, Predicates, and Axiomatic Method 27
   Proving an Implication and "If and Only If" 28
   Proof by Cases and Contradiction 29
   Number theory 30

Divisibility 31
Prime numbers 32
Modular arithmetic 33

Chapter 1 Exercises and More 34
Practice questions 34
Key takeaways 34
Answers to the practice questions 35
Project work 37
Projet help 37
Mathematical symbols and notations 38
Revisions (Flashcard topics) 38

CHAPTER 2 41

Discrete Mathematics And Algorithms 43

Set Theory 44
Sets, subsets, and power sets 44
Set operations (union, intersection, difference, complement) 44
Venn diagrams and set identities 45
Cartesian product of sets 45
Countable and uncountable sets 46

Logic and Propositional Calculus 47
Propositions and logical connectives 47
Logical equivalence and logical implications 48
Tautologies and contradictions 48
Rules of inference and proof techniques 48
Quantifiers (universal and existential) 49

Combinatorics and Counting Principles 50
Combinatorics 50
Permutations and combinations 51
The pigeonhole principle 52
Binomial coefficients 52
Inclusion-exclusion principle 53

Graph Theory 54

    Graphs, vertices, and edges 55
    Graph representations 55
    Types of Graphs 56
    Graph representations 58
    Graph properties 59
    Graph algorithms 59

Discrete Probability 61
    Sample spaces and events 61
    Probability rules and axioms 61
    Conditional probability and independence 61
    Bayes' theorem 62
    Random variables and probability distributions 62

Recursion and Recurrence Relations 64
    Recursive algorithms and functions 64
    Recurrence relations and their solutions 64
    Master theorem for solving recurrences 65
    Generating functions for solving recurrences 65

Number Theory 66
    Divisibility and modular arithmetic 66
    GCD and LCM 66
    Prime numbers and factorisation 66
    Diophantine equations 67
    Congruences and residues 67

Finite Automata and Formal Languages 68
    Deterministic Finite Automata (DFA) 68
    Nondeterministic Finite Automata (NFA) 68
    Regular Expressions 68
    Pushdown Automata 69

Algorithms and Data Structures 70
    Overview of algorithms and their characteristics 70
    Algorithm complexity and big-O notation 70
    Data structures used in computing 70
    Searching algorithms 71

    Sorting algorithms 72

Chapter 2 exercises and more 73
    Practice questions 73
    Key takeaways 74
    List of symbols from chapter 2 75
    Answers to the practice questions 76

CHAPTER 3 79

Linear Algebra and Calculus 81

Liner Algebra 82
    Scalars, vectors, and matrices 84
    Matrix operations 84
    Transpose of a matrix 85
    Identity and inverse matrices 85
    Systems of linear equations and Gaussian elimination 85
    Rank of a matrix 85
    Determinants and their properties 85
    Cramer's rule for solving linear systems 86
    Vector spaces and their properties 86
    Subspaces and bases 86
    Linear transformations and their properties 86
    Kernel and image of a linear transformation 86
    Eigenvectors and eigenvalues 87
    Diagonalisation of a matrix 87
    Orthogonality and Gram-Schmidt process 87

Calculus 88
    Differential Calculus 89
    Integral Calculus: 89
    Functions and their Graphs 90
    Limits and Continuity 90
    Limit Laws 90
    Continuity 91
    Definition of Derivative 91
    Rules for Differentiation 91

    Applications of Derivatives 91
    Higher-order Derivatives 92
    Integration... 92
    Rules for Integration 92
    Applications of Integrals 92
    Differential Equations 93

Chapter 3 exercises and more 94
    Practice questions 94
    Key takeaways 95
    Symbols used in this chapter 96
    Answers to the practice questions 97

CHAPTER 4 99

Probability and Statistics 101

Probability 103
    Sample Space and Types of Events.................................... 103
    Basic Properties of Probability 104
    Addition Rule and Mutually Exclusive Events 104
    Multiplication Rule and Independent Events 104
    Conditional Probability and Dependent Events 104
    Bayes' Theorem 105
    Complementary Events and Probability........................... 105
    Random Variables and Distributions 105
    Deviation from the Mean 106
    Random Walks... 106
    Theoretical and Experimental Probability 106
    Axiomatic Probability.. 106
    Law of Large Numbers 107

Statistics 108

Descriptive Statistics 109
    Measures of Central Tendency 109
    Measures of Dispersion... 109
    Measures of Association 110

 Graphical Representation of Data..*110*

Data Handling and Presentation 112
 Frequency Distribution Table...*112*
 Relative Frequency *112*
 Five Number Summary *112*
 Ungrouped and Grouped Data *113*

Probability Distributions 114
 Discrete Probability Distributions *114*
 Continuous Probability Distributions *115*
 Empirical Rule and Degree of Freedom *115*

Sampling and Sampling Distributions 117
 Population and Sample.. *117*
 Simple Random Sampling *117*
 Stratified Sampling... *117*
 Systematic Sampling *118*
 Central Limit Theorem *118*

Confidence Intervals and Hypothesis Testing.................. 119
 Confidence Interval for a Mean and Proportion *119*
 Comparing Two Means and Proportions............................. *119*
 Null and Alternative Hypotheses.. *119*
 Type I and Type II Errors.. *120*
 Significance Level and P-value *120*
 One-sample and Two-sample Tests *120*
 Categorical Data and Chi-square Test.................................. *120*

Regression Analysis 121
 Simple Linear Regression *121*
 Multiple Linear Regression *121*
 Coefficient of Determination (R-squared) *121*
 Non-parametric Statistics.. *121*
 Mann-Whitney U Test..*122*
 Kruskal-Wallis Test..*122*

Chapter 4 exercises and more.. 123

Practice questions 123
Key takeaways 124
Answers to the practice questions 125
Symbols to remember 127

CHAPTER 5 129

Optimisation and Applications of Mathematics 131

Optimisation 132

Local optimum 132
Global optimum 133

Linear Programming and Its Applications 134

Dual Linear Programming 135
Integer Linear Programming 135
Mixed-Integer Linear Programming 135
Multi-objective Linear Programming 136

Nonlinear Optimisation 137

Unconstrained Nonlinear Optimisation 138
Multi-objective Nonlinear Optimisation 138
Global Optimisation 139

Optimisation Algorithms 140

Tabu Search 141
Ant Colony Optimisation (ACO) 141
Hill Climbing 141
Differential Evolution (DE) 142

Mathematical Modelling in Computing 143

Machine Learning and Statistical Modelling 143
Optimisation in Machine Learning 144

Applications of Mathematical Concepts and Techniques in Various Fields 146

Cryptography 146
Image processing 147
Machine learning 147

Chapter 5 exercises and more 149
    Practice questions 149
    Key takeaways 149
    Symbols to remember 151
    Answer to the practice question 151

CHAPTER 6 153

Introduction to Boolean Algebra and Its Use in Digital Logic Circuits 155
    Boolean operators and their truth tables 156
        AND Operator 156
        Truth table for AND 156
        OR Operator 156
        Truth table for OR 156
        NOT Operator 157
        Truth table for NOT 157
    De Morgan's laws 157
        De Morgan's First Law 157
        De Morgan's Second Law 158
    Logic gates and their symbols 159
        AND Gate 159
        OR Gate 159
        NOT Gate (Inverter) 159
        NAND Gate 159
        NOR Gate 160
        XOR Gate (Exclusive OR) 160
        XNOR Gate (Exclusive NOR) 160
    Boolean expressions and their simplification 161
        Basic Boolean Operations 161
        Laws of Boolean Algebra 161
        Simplification Techniques 161
    Logic Gates and Their Use in Creating Complex Circuits 163
        Basic Logic Gates 163
        Derived Logic Gates 163
        Symbols of Logic Gates 164

- *Creating Complex Circuits* 164
- *Example of a Complex Circuit* 164
- *Combinational Logic Circuits* 165
- *Sequential Logic Circuits* 165
- *Flip-Flops and Latches* 165

Cryptography and Its Basics 167
- *History of Cryptography* 167
- *Cryptographic Primitives* 167
- *Cryptanalysis and Its Methods* 168
- *Cryptography Standards and Protocols* 168

Symmetric and Asymmetric Encryption 169
- *Symmetric Encryption Algorithms (e.g., DES, AES):* 169
- *Stream Ciphers and Block Ciphers* 169
- *Key Management and Distribution* 170
- *Asymmetric Encryption Algorithms (e.g., RSA, ECC)* 170

RSA Encryption Algorithm (move to crypto) 171
- *Secure Online Transactions:* 172
- *Email Encryption* 172
- *Secure Messaging Apps* 172
- *Password Protection* 172

Public Key Infrastructure and Digital Certificates 173
- *Public Key Infrastructure (PKI) and Its Components* 173
- *Certificate Authorities (CAs)* 173
- *Digital Certificates and Their Formats* 173
- *Certificate Revocation and Validation* 174

Machine Learning and Its Applications in Computing 175
- *Supervised Learning and Its Algorithms* 175
- *Unsupervised Learning and Its Algorithms* 175
- *Reinforcement Learning and Its Applications* 176
- *Deep Learning and Its Neural Network Architectures* 176

Supervised and Unsupervised Learning Algorithms 178
- *Regression Algorithms* 178
- *Classification Algorithms* 178
- *Clustering Algorithms* 179
- *Dimensionality Reduction Algorithms* 179

    Neural Networks and Deep Learning 181
        Feedforward Neural Networks... *181*
        Convolutional Neural Networks (CNNs) *181*
        Recurrent Neural Networks (RNNs)..................................... *181*
        Deep Learning Frameworks... *182*

Chapter 6 exercises and more................................ 183
    Practice questions *183*
    Key takeaways from this chapter *184*
    Symbols and notions *185*
    Further studies and resources *186*
    Answers to the practice questions *187*

Index... 191

Table of Figures.. 199

Other books in this series 200

About the author 201

Notes and references 203

INTRODUCTION

Welcome to Book 2 of the series on Computer Science for non-Computer Science Engineering Enthusiasts. In Book 1 (***Introduction To Computer Systems And Software Engineering***), we covered various topics related to computer systems, hardware, software, operating systems, computer networks, cloud computing, edge computing, usability and interaction, software engineering, programming languages, and web development. We hope you found the material in Book 1 useful and informative.

Mathematics is an integral part of computing, and this book, "***Introduction to Mathematics for Computing***", covers a range of mathematical concepts and techniques fundamental to the field. The book is designed to help non-CSE students enhance their mathematical skills and support their computing and data science studies.

The first chapter introduces the basic mathematical concepts relevant to computing, such as sets, sequences, series, functions, and relations. It covers the logical foundations of mathematics, such as propositions, predicates, and axiomatic methods. It also explains how to prove an implication and "if and only if" using proof by cases and contradiction. The chapter discusses number theory, divisibility, prime numbers, and modular arithmetic.

The second chapter covers discrete mathematics and algorithms, including set theory, logic, combinatorics, graph theory, discrete probability, recursion and recurrence relations, finite automata and formal languages, and algorithms and data structures. It explains the basic properties of sets, subsets, power sets, set operations, logical connectives and their truth tables, permutations and combinations, and graph representations, properties, algorithms, and types.

The third chapter covers linear algebra and calculus, including scalars, vectors, and matrices, matrix operations, systems of linear equations, determinants, eigenvectors and eigenvalues, vector spaces, bases, linear transformations, kernel and image, diagonalisation, orthogonality and Gram-Schmidt process, functions and their graphs, limits and continuity, derivatives, integrals, differential equations, and partial derivatives.

The fourth chapter covers probability and statistics, including sample space, events, probability rules and axioms, random variables and distributions, deviation from the mean, random walks, descriptive statistics, measures of central tendency, dispersion and association, graphical representation of data, probability distributions, empirical rule, degree of freedom, sampling and sampling distributions, confidence intervals and hypothesis testing, categorical data and chi-square test, regression analysis, and non-parametric statistics.

The fifth chapter covers optimisation and applications of mathematics, including local and global optimum, linear programming and its applications, nonlinear optimisation, multi-objective optimisation, optimisation algorithms, tabu search, ant colony optimisation, hill climbing, differential evolution, mathematical modelling in computing, and machine learning and statistical modelling.

The final chapter covers Boolean algebra and its use in digital logic circuits, including Boolean operators and their truth tables, De Morgan's laws, logic gates and their symbols, Boolean expressions and their simplification, basic and derived logic gates, complex circuits, combinational and sequential logic circuits, flip-flops and latches, cryptography and its basics, symmetric and asymmetric encryption, symmetric encryption algorithms such as DES and AES, RSA encryption algorithm, secure online transactions, email encryption, and public key infrastructure and digital certificates.

Each chapter includes practice questions, key takeaways, and answers to the practice questions. The book also provides project work and project help for students to apply the concepts they learn in real-world scenarios.

In summary, "*Introduction to Mathematics for Computing*" is a comprehensive book covering various mathematical topics relevant to computing and data science. It provides clear explanations and examples of each concept and technique, making it an essential resource for students who want to improve their mathematical skills and succeed in their computing and data science studies.

WHO IS THIS BOOK FOR?

This book, "Introduction to Mathematics for Computing," is primarily intended for students interested in gaining a foundational understanding of computer science and engineering but may not have a background in CSE. It is designed for students in their first year of university or who have completed their A-levels with a background in a non-CSE field, such as ICT.

The book is also useful for professionals looking to expand their computer science and engineering knowledge to help them succeed. For example, someone in marketing or finance may benefit from a better understanding of data analytics or cybersecurity.

This book is written for anyone who wants to learn computer science and engineering fundamentals and see how they apply them to other disciplines. The book is written in a way that makes the principles discussed in each chapter easy to learn and implement by providing a range of practice questions, project work, key takeaways, further study guidance and more.

WHAT WILL YOU LEARN IN THIS BOOK?

- Foundations of mathematical structures in computing, including sets, sequences, functions, and binary relations.
- The logical foundations of mathematics for computing include propositions, predicates, and the axiomatic method.
- Number theory, including divisibility, prime numbers, and modular arithmetic.

- Discrete mathematics and algorithms, including set theory, logic and propositional calculus, combinatorics, graph theory, discrete probability, recursion and recurrence relations, and formal languages.
- Linear algebra and calculus, including scalars, vectors, matrices, linear transformations, eigenvectors, eigenvalues, and differential and integral calculus.
- Probability and statistics, including basic probability concepts, random variables and distributions, sampling and sampling distributions, and hypothesis testing.
- Optimisation techniques, including linear programming, non-linear optimisation, and global optimisation algorithms.
- Cryptography and its basics, including symmetric and asymmetric encryption, digital certificates, and public key infrastructure.
- Machine learning and its applications in computing, including supervised and unsupervised learning algorithms, deep learning neural network architectures, and deep learning frameworks.

CHAPTER 1

INTRODUCTION TO MATHEMATICS FOR COMPUTING

Mathematics is an essential component of computing and programming, as it provides the fundamental tools needed to solve problems and create efficient algorithms. Whether designing a new software program, analysing data, or developing cutting-edge technologies, understanding the principles of mathematics is essential.

In computing, mathematics provides a foundation for problem-solving and programming concepts. For example, to create an algorithm that efficiently sorts a large dataset, one must understand mathematical concepts such as logarithmic time complexity and the efficiency of comparison-based sorting algorithms.

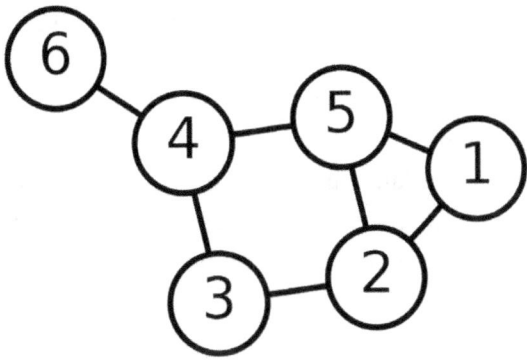

Figure 1 - Graphs such as these are among the objects studied by discrete mathematics[2]

Let's say; you are wondering how computers can quickly search through massive amounts of data; you can thank mathematical concepts like binary arithmetic and algorithms for searching and sorting.

In addition to being a fundamental component of computer science, mathematics is also used in many areas of computing, including cryptography, machine learning, and optimisation. Understanding mathematical concepts is crucial to success in these fields, as they require the ability to solve complex problems and create innovative solutions.

Mathematics for computing covers various topics, including sets, relations, functions, graphs, number theory, probability, and statistics. It also includes subjects such as linear algebra, calculus, and optimisation, which are used extensively in computer science.

While mathematics provides the theoretical foundations for computing, including algorithms, data structures, and complexity analysis, at the same time, computing has become an essential tool for mathematical research, enabling mathematicians to tackle complex problems and perform large-scale computations. For example, computer simulations are often used to model complex systems in physics, engineering, and other fields. In contrast, numerical methods and data analysis techniques are used to analyse and interpret experimental data. Additionally, computer algebra systems and symbolic computation tools have become increasingly crucial in mathematical research, allowing mathematicians to perform computations and verify the correctness of results that would be difficult or impossible to do by hand.

Whether you are planning to pursue a career in computer science or simply want to understand how computers work, studying mathematics for computing is essential. Mastering the fundamentals of mathematical concepts and problem-solving techniques, you will be better equipped to tackle complex problems and create innovative solutions that can transform the computing world.

DEFINITIONS

Mathematics for computing is a specialised field focusing on the mathematical concepts and methods used in computer science and engineering. It is essential for designing and analysing algorithms, modelling complex systems, and developing software applications. Mathematics for computing encompasses a range of mathematical topics, including logic, sets, relations, functions, graph theory, number theory, calculus, linear algebra, and probability.

One use case of mathematics for computing is in cryptography. Cryptography involves the secure transmission of information over the internet and relies heavily on mathematical concepts such as number theory and modular arithmetic. For example, the RSA encryption algorithm, widely used for secure communication, depends on the mathematical properties of large prime numbers and modular arithmetic.

Another case of mathematics used in computing is in data analysis and machine learning. These fields require a deep understanding of linear algebra, probability theory, and calculus. For example, linear algebra is used extensively in machine learning for tasks such as image recognition and natural language processing. Probability theory is also essential for developing statistical models and making predictions based on data.

A third use case of mathematics for computing is in computer graphics and game development. These fields rely heavily on mathematical concepts such as geometry, trigonometry, and calculus. For example, 3D graphics engines use linear algebra and trigonometry to manipulate objects in 3D space, while physics engines use calculus to model the behaviour of objects in a game world.

Those who want computer science or engineering careers should devote significant time to learning the relevant mathematics for computing. It equips its students with the theoretical grounding necessary for creating software, analysing data, and tackling complex issues in various disciplines.

Mathematical Foundations

Mathematical Foundations for Computing is a broad area of study focusing on the mathematical concepts and principles underpinning computing. To understand the role of mathematics in computing, it is important to have a basic understanding of some fundamental mathematical concepts. These concepts are essential for building the algorithms and systems that power modern computing applications.

One important concept is set theory, which is the study of collections of objects. Sets are fundamental mathematical building blocks and are used extensively in computing. They represent data structures, such as arrays and lists, and describe the relationships between different entities in a system.

Another essential concept is logic, which studies reasoning and argumentation. Logic provides the formal tools for reasoning about the correctness of computer programs and algorithms. It is also used to develop artificial intelligence and machine learning algorithms.

Number theory is also an important area of mathematics for computing. It is the study of the properties of numbers and their relationships to one another. It is used extensively in cryptography, the science of secure communication. Cryptography protects sensitive data, such as financial transactions and personal information, from unauthorised access.

Linear algebra is another critical area of mathematics for computing. It is the study of linear equations and their solutions. Linear algebra is used extensively in computer graphics, image and signal processing, and machine learning.

Calculus is an important area of mathematics for computing. It is the study of rates of change and accumulation and provides mathematical tools for understanding and optimising complex systems. Calculus is used extensively in fields such as physics, engineering, and economics, and it has many applications in computing.

Let's look at some examples for our clear understanding

Set theory:
The set theory provides a foundation for understanding and manipulating collections of objects, which is essential for organising and manipulating data in computing.

Boolean algebra:
Boolean algebra provides a framework for working with logical statements and operations, which is necessary for programming and creating digital circuits.

Number theory:
Number theory is a branch of mathematics that studies the properties of numbers, particularly integers. This field provides the basis for modern cryptography and data encryption.

Graph theory:
Graph theory provides a way to represent and analyse relationships between objects, which is important for modelling and solving problems in computer networks, social networks, and other applications.

Calculus:
Calculus provides a framework for studying change and rates of change, which is important for optimising algorithms and analysing large data sets.

We will look into those in more detail later in this book.

BASIC MATHEMATICAL CONCEPTS FOR COMPUTING

Basic Mathematical Concepts for Computing refer to the fundamental mathematical principles essential for solving problems and developing algorithms in computing. These concepts include arithmetic operations, number systems, algebraic expressions, and functions. Additionally, concepts such as sets, sequences, and binary relations play a vital role in developing data structures used in computing. A strong understanding of these mathematical concepts is necessary for effective problem-solving and developing efficient algorithms that can be implemented in software applications.

These concepts are used to develop algorithms, data structures, and programming languages. Some of the basic mathematical concepts used in computing include:

Sets:
A set is a collection of distinct objects. Sets represent data structures such as lists, arrays, and trees.

Relations:
A relation is a mathematical concept that connects two or more sets. In computing, relations define data structures and algorithms that operate on them.

Functions:
A function is a mathematical rule that maps input values to output values. In computing, functions are used to develop algorithms that process data.

Logic:
Logic is a branch of mathematics that deals with reasoning and argumentation. In computing, logic develops algorithms that make decisions based on specific conditions.

Probability:
Probability is the study of the likelihood of events occurring. In computing, probability is used to develop algorithms that make decisions based on probabilities.

These concepts provide the basis for understanding more complex mathematical concepts used in computing, such as calculus, linear algebra, and discrete mathematics. By understanding these basic mathematical concepts, non-technical students can gain an appreciation for how mathematics is used in computing and its importance in developing technology.

Foundations of Mathematical Structures in Computing

The Foundations of Mathematical Structures section will cover the fundamental concepts of sets, sequences, functions, and binary relations, which are essential mathematical structures in computer science. Sets are collections of objects or elements, and they play a significant role in the representation of data and the analysis of algorithms. Sequences are ordered lists of objects or elements, often used to represent data in a specific order, such as time or a sequence of events. Functions are mathematical objects that assign an output to every input, and they are used to model real-world phenomena and compute results.

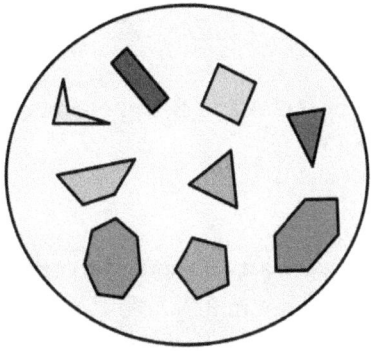

Figure 2 - A set of polygons in an Euler diagram[3]

Sets

In mathematics, a set is a collection of distinct objects, considered an object in its own right. These objects are usually referred to as elements or members of the set. Sets can be defined by listing their elements or using a rule or property to determine which objects belong to the set. Sets are fundamental mathematical concepts used to model various mathematical and real-world phenomena. They are also important tools in computer science, particularly in data structures and algorithms.

A set is a well-defined collection of objects or elements that are distinct from each other. These objects or elements can be anything from numbers to letters to colours and are enclosed in curly braces. For example, the set of all even numbers less than 10 can be denoted as {2, 4, 6, 8}.

SET OPERATIONS

Set operations refer to the actions that can be performed on sets. The three most common set operations are union, intersection, and difference.

Union:
The union of two sets A and B, denoted as A ∪ B, is the set of all elements in either A or B or both.

The intersection:
The intersection of sets A and B, denoted as A ∩ B, is the set of all elements in both A and B.

The difference:
The difference between sets A and B, denoted as A \ B or A − B, is the set of all elements in A but not in B.

The complement of a set A, denoted as A', is the set of all elements that are not in A but are in the universal set. The universal set is the set that contains all possible elements. For example, if the universal set is the set of all natural numbers, then the complement of all even numbers would be the set of all odd numbers.

SUBSETS AND POWER SETS

Subsets and power sets are important concepts in set theory, which is a branch of mathematics that deals with the study of collections of objects. A subset is a set that contains only elements that are also in another set, called the superset. For example, {2, 4} is a subset of {1, 2, 3, 4, 5} because both 2 and 4 are elements of both sets. We write this as {2, 4} ⊆ {1, 2, 3, 4, 5}.

The power set of a set is the set of all possible subsets of that set. For example, the power set of {1, 2, 3} is {{}, {1}, {2}, {3}, {1,2}, {1,3}, {2,3}, {1,2,3}}. The empty set and the original set itself are always included in the power set. The number of elements in a power set of a set with n elements is 2^n.

Subsets and power sets are useful in various mathematical applications, including probability theory, combinatorics, and set theory. In computer science, they are also used to study algorithms, data structures, and databases. For example, in database design, a power set is used to generate all possible combinations of attributes that can be used to index and search for data.

CARTESIAN PRODUCT OF SETS

The Cartesian product of two sets A and B, denoted by A × B, is the set of all ordered pairs (a, b) where a ∈ A and b ∈ B. In other words, it is the set of all possible combinations of elements from A and B.

For example, if A = {1, 2} and B = {3, 4}, then A × B = {(1, 3), (1, 4), (2, 3), (2, 4)}. The first element in each ordered pair is from A, while the second element is from B.

The Cartesian product can also be extended to more than two sets. For instance, if A = {1, 2}, B = {3, 4}, and C = {5, 6}, then A × B × C is the set of all ordered triples (a, b, c) where a ∈ A, b ∈ B, and c ∈ C.

Cartesian product is a fundamental concept in mathematics and computer science, and it has various applications, including database design, programming languages, and graph theory.

SEQUENCES AND SERIES

Sequences and series are important mathematical concepts that are used extensively in computing. A sequence is an ordered list of numbers or objects. Each element in the sequence is identified by its position or index. A series is the sum of the terms in a sequence.

Arithmetic and geometric sequences are two of the most common sequences used in computing. An arithmetic sequence is a sequence in which each term is obtained by adding a fixed number, called the common difference, to the preceding term. For example, 1, 3, 5, 7, 9 is an arithmetic sequence with a common difference of 2. A geometric sequence is a sequence in which each term is obtained by multiplying the preceding term by a fixed number, called the common ratio. For example, 2, 4, 8, 16, 32 is a geometric sequence with a common ratio of 2.

Series are important in computing as they are used to approximate functions and solve problems in numerical analysis. The convergence of a series is a key concept in calculus and is used to determine if the series sums to a finite value or if it diverges to infinity. Convergent series are used to approximate functions and solve numerical problems. There are several tests for convergence, such as the ratio test, the root test, and the integral test.

In computing, sequences and series are used in a wide range of applications, including cryptography, data compression, and signal processing. They are also used in the design and analysis of algorithms, especially in the analysis of the time and space complexity of algorithms. Understanding sequences and series is essential for any computer scientist or engineer working in these areas.

DEFINITION OF SEQUENCES

In mathematics, a sequence is an ordered list of elements that a set of natural numbers can index. In other words, it is a function whose domain is the set of natural numbers. The individual elements in a sequence are called terms, and they can be of any type, such as numbers, letters, or other objects.

For example, the sequence (a_n) can be defined as follows: $a_1 = 1$, $a_2 = 3$, $a_3 = 5$, $a_4 = 7$, and so on. The nth term of the sequence is denoted as a_n, and can be calculated using the formula $a\_n = 2n - 1$ for all n greater than or equal to 1.

Sequences are commonly used in many mathematics and computer science areas, such as number theory, calculus, and algorithms. They also represent data in various applications, such as time series analysis, signal processing, and cryptography.

The study of sequences involves analysing their properties and behaviour, such as convergence, divergence, and oscillation. It also involves developing methods for finding explicit formulas or recursion relations for sequences and proving theorems about their behaviour and properties.

ARITHMETIC AND GEOMETRIC SEQUENCES

Arithmetic and geometric sequences are two types of sequences commonly used in mathematics and computer science.

An arithmetic sequence is a sequence of numbers where each term is obtained by adding a fixed number to the previous term. The fixed number is called the common difference, denoted by d. The general form of an arithmetic sequence is:

a, a + d, a + 2d, a + 3d, ...

where a is the first term of the sequence, for example, the sequence 2, 5, 8, 11, 14 is an arithmetic sequence with a first term of 2 and a common difference of 3.

A geometric sequence is a sequence of numbers where each term is obtained by multiplying the previous term by a fixed number. The fixed number is called the common ratio, denoted by r. The general form of a geometric sequence is:

a, ar, ar^2, ar^3, ...

where a is the first term of the sequence, for example, the sequence 3, 6, 12, 24, 48 is a geometric sequence with a first term of 3 and a common ratio of 2.

Both arithmetic and geometric sequences have important applications in computer science and engineering, such as in algorithms and data structures. They also appear in various mathematical models, such as finance and physics.

SERIES AND CONVERGENCE

In mathematics, a series is the sum of the terms of a sequence. More formally, a series is a summation of the terms of an infinite sequence or a finite sequence. A finite series is simply the sum of the terms of a finite sequence, while an infinite series is the limit of the sum of the terms of an infinite sequence.

The convergence of a series is a measure of whether the series has a finite sum or not. A series is said to converge if the sum of its terms approaches a finite value as the number of terms increases, while a series is said to diverge if the sum of its terms approaches infinity or negative infinity.

Determining whether a series converges or diverges is a fundamental problem in calculus and analysis. Several tests can be used to determine the convergence or divergence of a series, such as the ratio, root, and comparison tests.

Series and convergence are important concepts in computing, as they are used in analysing algorithms and calculating numerical approximations. Understanding the convergence of a series is essential in many areas of computing, such as numerical analysis, scientific computing, and machine learning.

FUNCTIONS

A function is a rule that assigns to each element in a set (called the domain) exactly one element in another set (called the range or codomain). In simpler terms, a function is a relationship between two sets where every input has a unique output.

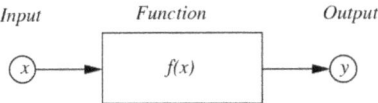

(a) One way of showing what a function does.

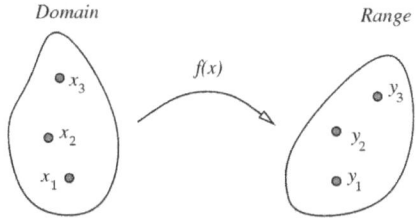

(b) A second way of showing what a function does.

Figure 3 - Visualising functions[4]

For example, the function f(x) = 2x takes an input value x and multiplies it by 2 to produce an output value. If we choose x = 3 as our input, the function's output would be 6.

Functions are represented in various ways, including algebraic expressions, graphs, and tables. They are essential in many areas of mathematics and computing, particularly in areas such as data analysis, optimisation, and machine learning.

There are many functions, including linear, quadratic, exponential, trigonometric, and logarithmic functions, each with unique properties and applications. Understanding functions is a fundamental concept in mathematics and is essential for understanding many aspects of computing and data analysis.

FUNCTION NOTATION AND DOMAIN AND RANGE

Function notation is a way of representing a function symbolically using variables and operations. It consists of an input, a process, and an output. The input is the independent variable, the process is the function rule, and the output is the dependent variable. Function notation is represented by a symbol "f" or "g" followed by an input variable "x," enclosed in parentheses. For example, $f(x) = 2x + 3$ represents a function that takes an input value of x and returns an output value of $2x + 3$.

Domain and range are important concepts in function notation. The domain of a function is the set of all possible input values for which the function is defined. The range of a function is the set of all possible output values that can be obtained from the function. In other words, the domain is the set of values for which the function can be evaluated, while the range is the set of values that the function can take.

For example, consider the function $f(x) = x^2$. The domain of this function is all real numbers because the function can be evaluated for any input value of x. However, the range of the function is all non-negative real numbers because the output value of the function can never be negative.

Understanding the domain and range of a function is important because it helps us determine its behaviour and suitability for certain applications.

Types of Functions: Injective, Surjective, and Bijective

Functions can be classified into different types based on their properties. Three common types of functions are:

Injective function:

An injective function (also known as a one-to-one function) maps distinct inputs to distinct outputs. In other words, each element in the domain is mapped to a unique element in the range. Formally, if $f(x_1) = f(x_2)$, then $x_1 = x_2$ for all x_1, x_2 in the domain. One example of an injective function is $f(x) = x + 1$, which maps each real number to a unique real number that is one unit greater than the input.

Surjective function:

A surjective function (also known as onto function) maps at least one element in the domain to every element in the range. In other words, every element in the range has at least one pre-image in the domain. Formally, if y is an element in the range, there exists an x in the domain such that f(x) = y. One example of a surjective function is f(x) = x^2, which maps every non-negative real number to a unique non-negative real number.

Bijective function:

A bijective function is both injective and surjective. It maps distinct inputs to distinct outputs and every element in the range has a unique pre-image in the domain. In other words, each element in the domain is mapped to a unique element in the range, and every element in the range has exactly one pre-image in the domain. Formally, if f(x1) = f(x2), then x1 = x2 for all x1, x2 in the domain, and if y is an element in the range, there exists a unique x in the domain such that f(x) = y. One example of a bijective function is f(x) = 2x + 1, which maps every real number to a unique real number that is twice the input plus one.

COMPOSITION OF FUNCTIONS

The composition of functions refers to the process of combining two or more functions to create a new function. When we compose two functions, we apply one function first and then apply the other function to the result of the first function. The composition of two functions f and g is denoted by (f o g) and is read as "f composed with g".

In other words, if we have two functions f(x) and g(x), then the composition of f and g can be defined as f(g(x)), which means we apply g to x first and then apply f to the result. The composition of functions is important in many areas of mathematics and computer science, as it allows us to combine different operations to create more complex functions.

For example, suppose we have a function f(x) = 2x + 1 and a function g(x) = x^2. If we want to find the composition of these two functions, we first apply g to x, which gives us g(x) = x^2. We then apply f to the result, which gives us f(g(x)) = f(x^2) = 2(x^2) + 1. This new function, f(g(x)), is the composition of the two original functions f(x) and g(x).

The composition of functions is used in many areas of computer science, including programming and data analysis. In programming, functions can be composed to create more complex programs that perform multiple operations. In data analysis, functions are composed to transform data and extract information from large datasets.

INVERSE FUNCTIONS

Inverse functions are functions that undo each other's effects. More specifically, a function f has an inverse function if there exists another function g such that g(f(x)) = x for all x in the domain of f and f(g(y)) = y for all y in the domain of g. The inverse function of f is usually denoted by f^-1.

For a function f to have an inverse function, it must be one-to-one, which means that no two distinct elements in its domain are mapped to the same element in its range. In other words, each element in the domain of f must correspond to a unique element in its range.

Finding the inverse of a function can be done using various methods, such as algebraic manipulation or graphing techniques. The inverse of a function can be used to solve equations involving the original function or to find the original input when the output is known.

Inverse functions have applications in many areas, such as computer graphics, cryptography, and engineering. For example, in cryptography, inverse functions are used to encrypt and decrypt messages in secure communication systems. In computer graphics, they are used to transform objects and images on a screen.

BINARY RELATIONS

Binary relations are a fundamental concept in mathematics and computer science. A binary relation is simply a set of ordered pairs. For example, the relation "is less than" on the set of real numbers is the set of all pairs (x, y) such that x is less than y.

Binary relations can be used to describe a wide variety of relationships between objects. For instance, in computer science, binary relations are often used to describe the relationship between objects in a database. In this context, the binary relation is often called a "relation" or a "table."

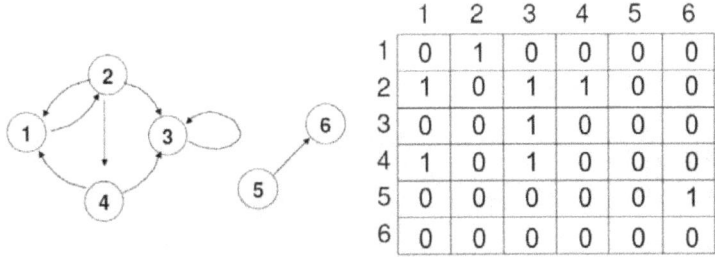

Figure 4 - A directed graph represented by an adjacency matrix[5]

One important type of binary relation is the equivalence relation. An equivalence relation is a binary relation that satisfies three properties: reflexivity, symmetry, and transitivity. For example, the relation "is congruent modulo 5" on the integers is an equivalence relation.

Another important type of binary relation is the partial order. A partial order is a binary relation that satisfies two properties: reflexivity and transitivity. For example, the relation "is a subset of" on the set of all sets is a partial order.

Binary relations can also be used to define functions. A function is a binary relation that satisfies two properties: every element in the domain is related to exactly one element in the range, and every element in the range is the image of at least one element in the domain.

PROPERTIES OF RELATIONS

In mathematics, a relation is a set of ordered pairs that shows a relationship between two sets. A binary relation is a relation between two sets, and it is usually denoted by a symbol such as "<", ">", "=", or "≤". In computing, binary relations are used to compare and relate data, such as in database management systems or in sorting algorithms.

Mathematics and computer science commonly study several important properties of binary relations. These properties help to classify and understand relations and can be useful in solving problems and designing algorithms.

Reflexivity:

A relation is reflexive if every element of the set is related to itself. For example, the relation "is equal to" is reflexive because every number is equal to itself. Formally, a relation R on a set A is reflexive if and only if for all a in A, (a,a) is in R.

Symmetry:

A relation is symmetric if, whenever (a,b) is in the relation, (b,a) is also in the relation. For example, the relation "is the same age as" is symmetric because if person A is the same age as person B, then person B is also the same age as person A. Formally, a relation R on a set A is symmetric if and only if for all a,b in A, if (a,b) is in R, then (b,a) is also in R.

Transitivity:

A relation is transitive if, whenever (a,b) and (b,c) are in the relation, then (a,c) is also in the relation. For example, the relation "is taller than" is transitive because if person A is taller than person B and person B is taller than person C, then person A is also taller than person C. Formally, a relation R on a set A is transitive if and only if for all a,b,c in A, if (a,b) and (b,c) are in R, then (a,c) is also in R.

Equivalence:

An equivalence relation is a relation that is reflexive, symmetric, and transitive. Equivalence relations partition a set into subsets, called equivalence classes, where elements in each class are related to each other but not to elements in other classes. For example, the relation "is congruent to modulo 3" is an equivalence relation on the set of integers because it is reflexive (every integer is congruent to itself), symmetric (if one integer is congruent to another, then the second integer is congruent to the first), and transitive (if one integer is congruent to another and the second integer is congruent to a third, then the first integer is congruent to the third).

EQUIVALENCE RELATIONS AND PARTITIONS

Equivalence relations and partitions are closely related mathematical concepts that arise in the study of binary relations. An equivalence relation is a binary relation that satisfies three conditions: reflexivity, symmetry, and transitivity. On the other hand, a partition is a way of dividing a set into non-empty subsets such that each element of the set is in exactly one of the subsets.

Equivalence relations can be used to define partitions. Given an equivalence relation on a set, the equivalence classes of the relation form a partition of the set. Conversely, any partition of a set induces an equivalence relation on the set, where two elements are related if and only if they belong to the same subset in the partition.

Equivalence relations and partitions are useful in many areas of mathematics, including algebra, topology, and set theory. Equivalence relations define quotient structures in algebra, such as groups, rings, and vector spaces. In topology, partitions are used to define open sets and closed sets. In set theory, partitions are used to define cardinality, which measures the size of sets.

Equivalence relations and partitions also have practical applications in computer science, such as in the study of algorithms and databases. For example, a database can be organised using a partitioning scheme that divides the data into non-overlapping subsets based on some equivalence relation on the data.

PARTIAL ORDER RELATIONS

A partial order relation is a binary relation that is reflexive, antisymmetric, and transitive. In other words, for any elements a, b, and c in a set S, a partial order relation satisfies the following conditions:

- Reflexivity: a is related to itself, i.e., a ≤ a.
- Antisymmetry: If a is related to b, and b is related to a, then a = b.
- Transitivity: If a is related to b, and b is related to c, then a is related to c.

Examples of partial order relations include the relation of less than or equal to on the set of real numbers and the relation of set inclusion on the set of all sets.

Partial order relations can define a hierarchy or ordering among elements of a set, where higher elements are related to lower elements. This can be used in various applications, such as task scheduling, database indexing, and computer network routing.

One important property of partial order relations is that they can be represented graphically as directed acyclic graphs, where the vertices represent the elements of the set and the directed edges represent the relation. This graph representation can be used to determine the transitive closure of the relation, which is the smallest transitive relation that contains the original relation.

LOGICAL FOUNDATIONS OF MATHEMATICS FOR COMPUTING

Logical Foundations of Mathematics for Computing refers to the study of the underlying logical structures and reasoning used in mathematics, which are fundamental to the field of computing. This includes using logical systems to formalise mathematical concepts and proofs and applying logic to the design and analysis of algorithms and computer programs.

At its core, the logical foundations of mathematics for computing involve using formal logic to define and reason mathematical concepts. This includes the use of propositional and predicate logic to formalise statements and proofs and axiomatic methods to establish the foundations of mathematical theories.

In computing, the logical foundations of mathematics play a crucial role in designing and analysing algorithms and computer programs. Logical reasoning is used to verify the correctness of algorithms and programs and to ensure that they operate as intended. This is particularly important in fields such as cryptography, where the security of algorithms and systems is critical.

PROPOSITIONS, PREDICATES, AND AXIOMATIC METHOD

Propositions, Predicates, and Axiomatic methods are the logical foundations of mathematics in computing. A proposition is a statement that is either true or false. A predicate is a statement that can be either true or false depending on the values of its variables. The axiomatic method is a way of building a logical system from a set of axioms or basic assumptions.

In computing, propositions and predicates define the conditions for executing a program or algorithm. For example, a proposition might be "x is greater than y," while a predicate might be "for all x and y, x is greater than y." Propositions and predicates can be combined using logical operators such as "and," "or," and "not" to create more complex conditions.

The axiomatic method builds mathematical systems from a set of axioms or basic assumptions. These axioms are assumed to be true without proof, and the system is built up using logical deductions based on these axioms. This method establishes the logical foundations of mathematical systems used in computing.

Propositions, predicates, and the axiomatic method are essential tools in developing and analysing algorithms, data structures, and other mathematical concepts used in computing. By using these logical foundations, programmers can ensure the correctness and efficiency of their programs, and mathematicians can develop and prove theorems about these concepts.

PROVING AN IMPLICATION AND "IF AND ONLY IF"

Proving an implication is a common mathematical technique to establish a cause-and-effect relationship between two statements. The symbol usually represents the implication "→". For example, let's say we have the two statements "If it is raining, then the ground is wet" and "It is raining." We can use the implication symbol to write this relationship as "It is raining → the ground is wet."

To prove this implication, we need to show that whenever the statement "It is raining" is true, the statement "The ground is wet" must also be true. In other words, we need to show that there is a causal relationship between the two statements. This can be done through deductive reasoning, using a combination of logic and known facts.

On the other hand, "if and only if" is a stronger form of implication, represented by the symbol "↔". This means that the two statements are causally related and logically equivalent. For example, the statement "Two triangles are congruent if and only if they have the same size and shape" can be represented as "Triangle A is congruent to Triangle B ↔ Triangle A and Triangle B have the same size and shape."

To prove an "if and only if" statement, we must prove both directions of the implication. In other words, we need to show that if the first statement is true, the second statement must also be true, and vice versa. This can be done using the same techniques as proving a regular implication but with the added step of proving the implication's converse (i.e., the second direction).

PROOF BY CASES AND CONTRADICTION

Proof by Cases is a common method of proof in mathematics that involves dividing a problem or statement into separate cases, then proving each case individually. This can often make it easier to approach a complex problem by breaking it down into smaller, more manageable parts. Here's a simple example:

Problem: Prove that the sum of two even numbers is always even.

Proof by Cases:
Case 1: Let a and b be two even numbers. Then we can write a = 2m and b = 2n, where m and n are integers. The sum of a and b is a + b = 2m + 2n = 2(m + n), which is also even. Therefore, the statement is true when a and b are both even.

Case 2: Let a be an even number and b be an odd number. Then we can write a = 2m and b = 2n + 1, where m and n are integers. The sum of a and b is a + b = 2m + 2n + 1 = 2(m + n) + 1, which is odd. Therefore, the statement is not true when a is even and b is odd.

Case 3: Let a and b be two odd numbers. Then we can write a = 2m + 1 and b = 2n + 1, where m and n are integers. The sum of a and b is a + b = 2m + 2n + 2 = 2(m + n + 1), which is even. Therefore, the statement is not true when a and b are both odd.

Since we have considered all possible cases, we can conclude that the sum of two even numbers is always even.

Proof by Contradiction is a method of proof that involves assuming the opposite of what we want to prove then showing that this assumption leads to a contradiction or absurdity. Here's an example:

Problem: Prove that the square root of 2 is irrational.

Proof by Contradiction:
Assume that the square root of 2 is rational, which means it can be expressed as a ratio of two integers: $\sqrt{2} = a/b$, where a and b have no common factors. We can assume that a and b are both positive, since the negative case can be handled similarly.

Squaring both sides, we get $2 = a^2/b^2$. Multiplying both sides by b^2, we get $2b^2 = a^2$. This means that a^2 is an even number, since it is twice some other number (b^2). Therefore, a itself must be even, since the square of an odd number is always odd.

If a is even, we can write $a = 2k$, where k is another integer. Substituting this into the equation $2b^2 = a^2$, we get $2b^2 = (2k)^2 = 4k^2$. Dividing both sides by 2, we get $b^2 = 2k^2$. This means that b^2 is even, and therefore b must also be even.

However, we assumed earlier that a and b had no common factors. If they are both even, then they must have a common factor of 2. This contradicts our assumption, so our original assumption that $\sqrt{2}$ is rational must be false. Therefore, $\sqrt{2}$ is irrational.

NUMBER THEORY

Number theory is the branch of mathematics that deals with the properties and behaviour of numbers, especially integers. It is concerned with the study of various properties of numbers such as divisibility, prime numbers, factorisation, and congruences.

For example, divisibility is an important concept in number theory. A number is said to be divisible by another number if it can be divided by that number without leaving a remainder. For instance, 12 is divisible by 3 since 12 ÷ 3 = 4, whereas 15 is not divisible by 3 since 15 ÷ 3 = 5 with a remainder of 0.

Another important concept in number theory is prime numbers. Prime numbers are numbers that are divisible only by 1 and themselves. For instance, 2, 3, 5, 7, 11, 13, and 17 are prime numbers.

The factorisation is another important concept in number theory, which involves expressing a given number as a product of other numbers. For example, the number 20 can be expressed as 2 × 2 × 5, which is its prime factorisation.

Congruences are also an important concept in number theory, which involve comparing the remainders of two numbers when divided by a given number. For example, $9 \equiv 3 \pmod{6}$, since both 9 and 3 leave the same remainder of 3 when divided by 6. Congruences have important applications in cryptography, which is the practice of secure communication.

Divisibility

Divisibility is a fundamental concept in number theory that refers to the ability of one number to be divided by another without leaving any remainder. When a number A is divisible by another number B, it means that A can be divided by B without leaving any remainder. In mathematical notation, we write it as A/B = Q where Q is a quotient that is a whole number.

For example, 12 is divisible by 3 because 12/3 = 4, and there is no remainder left. On the other hand, 14 is not divisible by 3 because 14/3 = 4 with a remainder of 2.

Divisibility has many important properties, and it is often used in number theory to solve problems related to prime numbers, factorisation, and modular arithmetic. One of the most important properties of divisibility is the division algorithm, which states that for any two positive integers A and B, there exist unique integers Q and R such that A = BQ + R, where R is the remainder and 0 <= R < B.

For example, if we want to divide 17 by 4, we can use the division algorithm to get 17 = 4*4 + 1, which means that 17 divided by 4 gives a quotient of 4 and a remainder of 1.

Divisibility is also related to prime numbers, which are positive integers greater than 1 with no positive integer divisors other than 1 and themselves. Prime numbers play a crucial role in number theory, and many important results in mathematics are based on the properties of prime numbers.

For example, the fundamental theorem of arithmetic states that every positive integer can be expressed uniquely as a product of prime numbers up to the order of the factors. This theorem is used in many areas of mathematics, including cryptography, where it is used to create secure encryption algorithms.

PRIME NUMBERS

Prime numbers are positive integers greater than 1 that have no positive integer divisors other than 1 and itself. For example, 2, 3, 5, 7, 11, and 13 are all prime numbers. Prime numbers are important in number theory and have many applications in computer science, including cryptography, coding theory, and prime factorisation algorithms.

Prime numbers have several interesting properties. For example, there are infinitely many prime numbers, and the distribution of prime numbers among the integers is unpredictable. The largest known prime number as of 2023 has over 24 million digits.

One common use of prime numbers in computer science is in public-key cryptography systems such as the RSA algorithm. In such systems, the security of the encryption relies on the fact that it is difficult to factor large composite numbers into their prime factors. Another use of prime numbers is in generating random numbers for use in cryptographic protocols and other applications where randomness is important.

In addition to their practical applications, prime numbers have fascinated mathematicians for centuries. The study of prime numbers is an active area of research in number theory, and many famous conjectures and open problems, such as the Riemann Hypothesis, are related to prime numbers.

MODULAR ARITHMETIC

Modular arithmetic is a branch of number theory that deals with integers and their remainders when divided by a fixed integer, called the modulus. In modular arithmetic, two integers are considered congruent if their difference is divisible by the modulus. This concept is denoted by the symbol "≡", which is read as "congruent to".

For example, if we consider the modulus 5, then $12 \equiv 2 \pmod{5}$, because their difference 10 is divisible by 5. Similarly, $27 \equiv 2 \pmod{5}$, because their difference 25 is divisible by 5.

Modular arithmetic has many applications in computer science, particularly in cryptography. One famous example is the RSA encryption algorithm, which is used to secure online transactions and communications. RSA relies heavily on modular arithmetic to encode and decode messages.

Another application of modular arithmetic is in computer graphics, where it is used to create repeating patterns and animations. The concept of a "tile" in computer graphics is closely related to modular arithmetic since it involves repeating a pattern in a grid-like fashion.

Chapter 1 Exercises and More

Below you will find a set of practice questions and their corresponding answers. In addition, this section includes key takeaways from the chapter and several project ideas to help reinforce your understanding of the material.

Practice Questions

1. Define a set and give an example of a finite and infinite set.
2. If A = {1, 2, 3} and B = {3, 4, 5}, find A ∪ B, A ∩ B, and A \ B.
3. What is the Cartesian product of A = {a, b} and B = {1, 2, 3}?
4. Define a sequence and give an example of an arithmetic and geometric sequence.
5. Define a function and give an example of an injective function but not a surjective.
6. Define a binary relation and give an example of a relation that is reflexive but not transitive.
7. What is the Inclusion-Exclusion Principle and how is it used to find the number of elements in the union of two or more sets?
8. What is a simple graph and give an example of a simple graph with five vertices and three edges?
9. Define a predicate and give an example of a true and false statement using the predicate "x is an even number."

Key Takeaways

- Mathematics plays a crucial role in computing, providing the foundation for many concepts and algorithms.
- Sets are collections of objects, and set theory provides the basis for many mathematical structures used in computing.

- Sequences and series are important mathematical concepts that can be used to model various phenomena in computing.
- Functions are fundamental to computer science and can be used to model relationships between sets.
- Binary relations are used to describe relationships between two sets, and they have important properties like reflexivity, symmetry, and transitivity.
- Equivalence and partial order relations are important binary relations types with unique properties.
- Combinatorics is the study of counting and can be used to solve problems related to probability, graph theory, and other areas of computing.
- Graph theory is a branch of mathematics that deals with the study of graphs and their properties, and it has many applications in computer science.
- Logical foundations of mathematics, such as propositions and predicates, are important for reasoning and proving theorems.

ANSWERS TO THE PRACTICE QUESTIONS

1. A set is a collection of distinct objects. An example of a finite set is the set of colours in a rainbow: {red, orange, yellow, green, blue, indigo, violet}. An example of an infinite set is the set of all positive integers: {1, 2, 3, 4, ...}.
2. $A \cup B = \{1, 2, 3, 4, 5\}$, $A \cap B = \{3\}$, $A \setminus B = \{1, 2\}$
3. The Cartesian product of A and B is the set of all ordered pairs (a, b) where $a \in A$ and $b \in B$. In this case, $A \times B = \{(a, 1), (a, 2), (a, 3), (b, 1), (b, 2), (b, 3)\}$.
4. A sequence is a list of numbers that follow a certain pattern. An example of an arithmetic sequence is {1, 3, 5, 7, 9, ...}, where each term is the sum of the previous term and a constant difference of 2. An example of a geometric sequence is {2, 4, 8, 16, 32, ...}, where each term is the product of the previous term and a constant ratio of 2.

5. A function is a rule that assigns each element in the domain to exactly one element in the range. An example of a function that is injective (one-to-one) but not surjective (onto) is $f(x) = x^3$, where the domain is all real numbers and the range is all real numbers greater than or equal to 0.
6. A binary relation is a set of ordered pairs that relate elements from two sets. An example of a reflexive but not transitive relation is the relation "is a sibling of" on the set of all people. The relation is reflexive because everyone is a sibling of themselves, but it is not transitive because if A is a sibling of B and B is a sibling of C, it does not necessarily mean that A is a sibling of C.
7. The Inclusion-Exclusion Principle states that the size of the union of two or more sets is equal to the sum of their sizes minus the size of their intersection, plus the size of the intersection of all possible pairs of sets, minus the size of the intersection of all possible triples of sets, and so on. It is used to find the number of elements in a complicated union of sets by breaking it down into simpler parts.
8. A simple graph is an undirected graph with no loops or multiple edges between any two vertices. An example of a simple graph with five vertices and three edges is shown below:

```css
o---o
|\ /|
| X |
|/ \|
o---o
```

9. A predicate is a statement that can be either true or false depending on the value of one or more variables. An example of a true statement using the predicate "x is an even number" is "2 is an even number," while an example of a false statement is "3 is an even number."

PROJECT WORK

1. Set operations and Venn diagrams: Create a program that can draw Venn diagrams for two or three sets and perform set operations such as union, intersection, and complement.
2. Number theory and modular arithmetic: Implement a program that can determine whether a given integer is prime or composite, and then use modular arithmetic to determine whether it is a quadratic residue modulo a given prime.
3. Graph theory and shortest path algorithms: Create a program that can read in a graph represented as an adjacency matrix or list, and then apply Dijkstra's algorithm to find the shortest path between two vertices.
4. Propositional logic and truth tables: Implement a program that can evaluate a given propositional formula using truth tables, and then determine whether it is a tautology or contradiction.
5. Functions and inverse functions: Create a program that can find the inverse of a given function and then use it to solve equations involving that function.

PROJET HELP

1. For the Venn diagram project, you could use a graphics library such as matplotlib or tkinter to draw the diagrams. You could also use sets from the Python standard library to perform the set operations.
2. For the number theory and modular arithmetic project, you could use the Miller-Rabin test to determine whether a given integer is prime. For the quadratic residue problem, you could use the Legendre symbol or the Jacobi symbol to determine whether a given integer is a quadratic residue modulo a given prime.

3. For the graph theory and shortest path project, you could use an adjacency list or matrix to represent the graph, and then use a priority queue to implement Dijkstra's algorithm.
4. For the propositional logic and truth tables project, you could use a library such as sympy to parse and evaluate the propositional formulas.
5. You could use the Newton-Raphson method to solve equations involving the inverse function for the functions and inverse functions project.

Mathematical Symbols and Notations

- ∪ and ∩ for the union and intersection of sets, respectively
- A \ B for the set difference of A and B
- f: A → B for a function f from set A to set B
- ≡ for congruence in modular arithmetic
- ∀ and ∃ for universal and existential quantifiers, respectively.

Revisions (Flashcard topics)

- If you want to revise chapter 1, please make flashcards of the below key topics:
- Arithmetic sequences: A sequence of numbers where each term is the sum of the previous term and a fixed constant.
- Binary relations: A relation between two sets, where each element in the first set is related to one or more elements in the second set.
- Bijective functions: A function where each element in the domain is paired with exactly one element in the range, and vice versa.
- Cartesian product: A set of ordered pairs formed by taking one element from each of two sets.
- Combinatorics: The study of counting and arranging objects.

- Composition of functions: A function that is created by combining two or more functions, where the output of one function is used as the input of another function.
- Divisibility: A property of integers that describes whether one integer can be evenly divided by another integer.
- Domain and range: The set of input values and output values, respectively, for a function.
- Equivalence relations: A relation that is reflexive, symmetric, and transitive.
- Finite sets: Sets that have a specific, finite number of elements.
- Function notation: A way to represent a function using symbols and variables.
- Geometric sequences: A sequence of numbers where each term is the product of the previous term and a fixed constant.
- Graph algorithms: Algorithms used to analyze and manipulate graphs.
- Graph representations: Ways to visually represent graphs.
- Inclusion-exclusion principle: A counting principle that allows for the calculation of the size of the union of two or more sets.
- Injective functions: A function where each element in the domain is paired with at most one element in the range.
- Modular arithmetic: A type of arithmetic that involves working with remainders when dividing by a fixed integer.
- Number theory: The study of integers and their properties.
- Partial order relations: A relation that is reflexive, antisymmetric, and transitive.
- Power sets: The set of all subsets of a given set.
- Predicates: Statements that describe a relationship between one or more variables.
- Prime numbers: A positive integer greater than 1 that has no positive integer divisors other than 1 and itself.

- Proofs by cases and contradiction: Methods of proof where the argument is divided into cases, or where the argument assumes the opposite of what is to be proven.
- Propositions: Statements that can be either true or false.
- Pigeonhole principle: A counting principle that states that if there are more pigeons than pigeonholes, then at least one pigeonhole must have more than one pigeon.
- Reflexive relations: A relation where each element in a set is related to itself.
- RSA encryption algorithm: A public-key cryptosystem used for secure communication.
- Sequences: An ordered list of numbers or other mathematical objects.
- Series: The sum of the terms in a sequence.
- Simple graphs: A graph where there is at most one edge between any two vertices.
- Subsets: A set that contains only elements that are also contained in another set.
- Surjective functions: A function where each element in the range is paired with at least one element in the domain.
- Transitive relations: A relation where if a is related to b, and b is related to c, then a is related to c.
- Types of functions: Different categories of functions, such as injective, surjective, and bijective.
- Types of graphs: Different categories of graphs, such as simple graphs and directed graphs.
- Union and intersection of sets: The set of all elements that belong to either both sets (union) or only to both sets (intersection).

CHAPTER 2

Discrete Mathematics And Algorithms

Discrete Mathematics is a branch of mathematics that deals with distinct or separate objects, as opposed to continuous mathematics, which focuses on continuous or infinite objects. It plays a crucial role in computer science, providing the foundation for understanding various fundamental concepts and principles in computing. In this chapter, we will explore the world of discrete mathematics and its applications in algorithms, which are step-by-step procedures for solving computational problems.

Algorithms are the backbone of computer science, enabling computers to perform complex tasks by following precise instructions. They can be thought of as recipes for solving problems, where each step must be executed in a specific order to achieve the desired outcome. An important aspect of algorithms is their efficiency, which is determined by the time and resources required to execute them. By understanding the principles of discrete mathematics, we can design and analyse algorithms to optimise their performance and make them suitable for various applications.

This chapter will introduce you to the key concepts of discrete mathematics, such as set theory, logic, combinatorics, graph theory, and more. You will also learn about different types of algorithms, their characteristics, and how to analyse their complexity. By the end of this chapter, you will have a solid understanding of the role of discrete mathematics in computer science and how it is applied to the development of efficient algorithms. Remember that this chapter is designed for non-CSE students, and we will strive to explain the concepts in an accessible and easy-to-understand manner. So let's dive into the fascinating world of discrete mathematics and algorithms!

SET THEORY

Set Theory is the branch of mathematics that studies sets, which are collections of distinct objects or elements. It is a fundamental concept in discrete mathematics and provides the basis for various other topics. This section will explore the basics of set theory, including sets, subsets, power sets, set operations, Venn diagrams, Cartesian products, and countable and uncountable sets.

SETS, SUBSETS, AND POWER SETS

A set is a collection of distinct objects called elements or members. Sets are usually denoted by capital letters, and their elements are enclosed in curly braces. For example, A = {1, 2, 3} is a set containing the elements 1, 2, and 3.

A subset is a set formed by selecting some or all elements of another set. If every element of set A is also an element of set B, then A is a subset of B, denoted by A ⊆ B. The empty set, represented by ∅, is a subset of every set.

A power set of a set A, denoted by P(A), is the set of all possible subsets of A, including the empty set and the set A itself. For example, if A = {1, 2}, then the power set P(A) = {∅, {1}, {2}, {1, 2}}.

SET OPERATIONS (UNION, INTERSECTION, DIFFERENCE, COMPLEMENT)

Set operations allow us to combine or manipulate sets in various ways. The main set operations are:

Union:
The union of two sets A and B, denoted by A ∪ B, is the set of all elements that belong to either A or B or both. For example, if A = {1, 2, 3} and B = {2, 3, 4}, then A ∪ B = {1, 2, 3, 4}.

Intersection:

The intersection of two sets A and B, denoted by A ∩ B, is the set of all elements that belong to both A and B. For example, if A = {1, 2, 3} and B = {2, 3, 4}, then A ∩ B = {2, 3}.

Difference:

The difference of two sets A and B, denoted by A - B, is the set of all elements that belong to A but not to B. For example, if A = {1, 2, 3} and B = {2, 3, 4}, then A - B = {1}.

Complement:

The complement of a set A, denoted by A', is the set of all elements that do not belong to A. The complement is usually defined with respect to a universal set U, which contains all elements under consideration. For example, if A = {1, 2, 3} and U = {1, 2, 3, 4}, then A' = {4}.

VENN DIAGRAMS AND SET IDENTITIES

Venn diagrams are visual representations of sets and their relationships. In a Venn diagram, sets are represented by closed shapes, usually circles, and their elements are placed inside the shapes. Overlapping regions indicate elements that are common to the sets.

Venn diagrams can help us understand and verify set identities, which are equations involving sets and set operations. Some common set identities include the distributive, commutative, and associative laws for union and intersection operations.

CARTESIAN PRODUCT OF SETS

The Cartesian product of two sets A and B, denoted by A × B, is the set of all possible ordered pairs (a, b) such that a ∈ A and b ∈ B. For example, if A = {1, 2} and B = {a, b}, then A × B = {(1, a), (1, b), (2, a), (2, b)}. The Cartesian product can be extended to more than two sets as well.

The Cartesian product is used in various applications, such as defining relations and functions between sets, and representing matrices and grids in mathematics and computing.

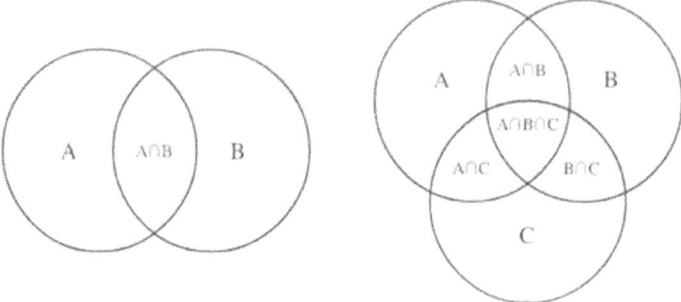

Figure 5 - A schematic diagram used in logic theory to depict collections of sets and represent their relationships[6]

COUNTABLE AND UNCOUNTABLE SETS

Sets can be classified as countable or uncountable based on the number of elements they contain. A set is countable if its elements can be put into one-to-one correspondence with the set of natural numbers (i.e., it can be counted). Countable sets include finite sets, such as {1, 2, 3}, and some infinite sets, such as the set of all even numbers.

Uncountable sets are sets that cannot be put into one-to-one correspondence with the set of natural numbers. They have a larger "size" or "cardinality" than countable sets. An example of an uncountable set is a set of all real numbers.

Understanding the difference between countable and uncountable sets is important in various areas of mathematics, including analysis and the study of infinite processes. In computer science, countable sets are particularly relevant, as they can be more easily processed and stored by computers than uncountable sets.

LOGIC AND PROPOSITIONAL CALCULUS

Logic is the study of reasoning and the principles that govern the validity of arguments. Propositional calculus, also known as propositional logic or statement logic, is a branch of logic that deals with propositions (statements that can be true or false) and the logical relationships between them. It provides a foundation for understanding various aspects of computer science, such as programming, circuit design, and artificial intelligence. This section will explore the basics of propositional calculus, including propositions, logical connectives, truth tables, logical equivalence, tautologies, contradictions, rules of inference, and quantifiers.

PROPOSITIONS AND LOGICAL CONNECTIVES

A proposition is a declarative statement that can be either true or false, but not both. Examples of propositions are "it is raining" and "2 + 2 = 4". Logical connectives are symbols that form compound propositions from simpler ones. The main logical connectives are:

Negation (NOT): ¬p, which means "not p"
Conjunction (AND): p ∧ q, which means "p and q"
Disjunction (OR): p ∨ q, which means "p or q"
Implication (IMPLIES): p → q, which means "if p, then q"
Biconditional (IFF): p ↔ q, which means "p if and only if q"
2.2. Truth tables

A truth table is a tabular representation of the truth values of a compound proposition for all possible combinations of truth values of its constituent propositions. Truth tables are used to determine propositions' logical properties and analyse arguments' validity.

Logical Equivalence and Logical Implications

Two propositions are logically equivalent if they have the same truth values for all possible combinations of truth values of their constituent propositions. Logical equivalence is denoted by p ≡ q. A logical implication is a relationship between two propositions where the truth of the first proposition (the antecedent) guarantees the truth of the second proposition (the consequent). The logical implication is denoted by p ⇒ q.

Tautologies and Contradictions

Tautologies and contradictions are important concepts in the study of logic, as they help determine propositions' logical properties and arguments' validity. A tautology is a proposition that is always true, regardless of the truth values of its constituent propositions. A contradiction is a proposition that is always false.

Rules of Inference and Proof Techniques

Rules of inference are logical patterns that allow us to deduce new propositions from given ones. Proof techniques are methods used to establish the truth of a proposition based on established rules of inference. Some common proof techniques are:

Direct proof: proving a proposition by a series of logical deductions from given premises or previously proven statements

Indirect proof: proving a proposition by assuming the opposite and showing that it leads to a contradiction

Proof by contradiction: proving a proposition by assuming its negation and showing that it leads to a contradiction

Proof by contrapositive: proving a proposition by proving its contrapositive, which is the statement formed by negating and reversing the antecedent and consequent of an implication

Quantifiers (Universal and Existential)

Quantifiers are used to express propositions involving variables and to specify the scope of these variables. There are two main types of quantifiers:

Universal quantifier (∀): "for all" or "every", used to express that a proposition is true for all elements in a given domain
Existential quantifier (∃): "there exists" or "some", used to express that a proposition is true for at least one element in a given domain.

For example, consider the following propositions:

"For all natural numbers x, x is greater than or equal to 0." This proposition can be written using the universal quantifier as "∀x (x ∈ N ⇒ x ≥ 0)".
"There exists a natural number x such that x is even." This proposition can be written using the existential quantifier as "∃x (x ∈ N ∧ x is even)".
Quantifiers can be combined and nested to express more complex propositions. For example, "For every natural number x, there exists a natural number y such that y is greater than x" can be written as "∀x ∃y (x ∈ N ∧ y ∈ N ∧ y > x)".

Understanding quantifiers and their use in logical expressions is essential in various areas of mathematics and computer science, such as the study of algorithms, formal languages, and formal methods for verifying software correctness. They also play a crucial role in predicate logic, a more expressive form of logic that extends propositional calculus by introducing variables and quantifiers.

Combinatorics and Counting Principles

Combinatorics and counting principles are branches of mathematics that deal with counting, arranging, and selecting objects from a set or a collection. These principles are crucial in various fields, such as computer science, statistics, and probability. They help us understand the structure and patterns of different arrangements and combinations.

Combinatorics

Combinatorics is a branch of mathematics that deals with counting, arranging, and selecting objects, such as combinations, permutations, and partitions. It has applications in various fields, including computer science, engineering, physics, and biology.

Combinatorics involves studying discrete structures and their properties, such as graphs, trees, and hypergraphs. It is concerned with finding the number of ways objects can be arranged or selected, given certain constraints and rules.

Some important topics in combinatorics include the following:

Combinations and permutations:
Combinations are the number of ways to select a subset of objects from a larger set, while permutations are the number of ways to arrange objects in a specific order.

Binomial coefficients:
These are numbers that appear in the expansion of binomials and represent the number of ways to select k objects from a set of n objects.

Pascal's triangle:
This triangular array of numbers contains binomial coefficients and has numerous mathematical and combinatorial properties.

Generating functions:
These functions encode information about a sequence of numbers, and they have applications in combinatorics, number theory, and other areas of mathematics.

Graph theory:
This is the study of graphs, which are mathematical structures consisting of vertices and edges. Graph theory has applications in computer science, optimisation, and social network analysis, among other fields.

PERMUTATIONS AND COMBINATIONS

Permutations and combinations are fundamental concepts in combinatorics. A permutation is an arrangement of objects in a specific order, while a combination is a selection of objects from a larger set without regard to order.

Permutations are used to count the number of possible ways to order a set of objects. For example, if you have three objects A, B, and C, the number of permutations of these objects is 3! (3 factorial), which is equal to 6. The six permutations are ABC, ACB, BAC, BCA, CAB, and CBA.

Conversely, combinations are used to count the number of ways to select a subset of objects from a larger set. For example, if you have four objects A, B, C, and D, and you want to select two of them, the number of combinations is 4 choose 2, which is equal to 6. The six combinations are AB, AC, AD, BC, BD, and CD.

Permutations and combinations have many applications in computer science, such as in cryptography, error-correcting codes, and network routing algorithms. They are also used in probability theory to calculate the number of possible outcomes of an experiment.

Introduction to Mathematics for Computing

THE PIGEONHOLE PRINCIPLE

The pigeonhole principle is a fundamental concept in combinatorics that states that if there are more items to place into containers than there are containers, then at least one container must contain more than one item. In other words, if n items are placed into m containers where n > m, then at least one container must contain more than one item.

This principle is often used to prove the existence of certain mathematical objects or phenomena. For example, it can be used to show that there must be two people in a large group of people with the same birthday or that in any set of five integers, there must be two whose sum is divisible by 2.

The pigeonhole principle has numerous applications in computer science, such as in algorithm design, data structures, and network protocols. For instance, it can be used to analyse the performance of hashing algorithms or to prove that certain communication protocols are secure.

In addition, the pigeonhole principle has implications in many other fields, such as physics, economics, and biology. For example, it can be used to analyse the behaviour of large populations or to prove certain statistical properties of physical systems.

Overall, the pigeonhole principle is a powerful tool in mathematics and computer science that helps to prove the existence of certain phenomena or to analyse the behaviour of systems with many variables.

BINOMIAL COEFFICIENTS

Binomial coefficients are an essential concept in combinatorics used to calculate the number of combinations of objects. The binomial coefficient, also known as the choose function, represents the number of ways to choose k objects out of n objects without replacement and order not mattering. It is denoted as ${n\choose k}$ or $\binom{n}{k}$.

The formula for the binomial coefficient is $\binom{n}{k} = \frac{n!}{k!(n-k)!}$, where n and k are non-negative integers and n is greater than or equal to k. The exclamation point denotes the factorial function, which is the product of all positive integers up to a given number.

For example, if we have a set of 5 objects and we want to choose 3 objects from it, the number of possible combinations would be $\binom{5}{3} = \frac{5!}{3!(5-3)!} = \frac{5 \times 4 \times 3}{3 \times 2 \times 1} = 10$. So, there are 10 ways to choose 3 objects from a set of 5 objects.

Binomial coefficients are used in various areas of mathematics, such as probability theory, algebra, and calculus. They are also applied in computer science for algorithm design and analysis, especially in the analysis of recursive algorithms.

INCLUSION-EXCLUSION PRINCIPLE

The inclusion-exclusion principle is a counting technique used in combinatorics to calculate the size of the union or intersection of sets. It states that the size of the union of two or more sets is equal to the sum of their individual sizes minus the size of their intersection. In mathematical notation, for two sets A and B, the principle can be expressed as:

$$|A \cup B| = |A| + |B| - |A \cap B|$$

The principle can be extended to more than two sets as follows:

$$|A_1 \cup A_2 \cup \ldots \cup A_n| = \Sigma |A_i| - \Sigma |A_i \cap A_j| + \Sigma |A_i \cap A_j \cap A_k| - \ldots + (-1)^{(n+1)} |A_1 \cap A_2 \cap \ldots \cap A_n|$$

where Σ represents the sum over all possible combinations of i, j, k, and so on, and $(-1)^{(n+1)}$ is a sign factor that alternates in sign for odd and even values of n.

The inclusion-exclusion principle is often used in problems related to probability and statistics, such as calculating the probability of at least one event occurring in a set of events. It is also used in various other fields, including computer science and economics.

GRAPH THEORY

Graph theory is a branch of mathematics that deals with the study of graphs and their properties. A graph is a mathematical structure that consists of a set of vertices (or nodes) and a set of edges (or lines) that connect these vertices. Graphs are widely used in computer science and engineering for modelling and solving real-world problems.

The study of graph theory involves analysing the properties of graphs, including their connectivity, planarity, colouring, and algorithms for traversing or finding paths between vertices. Graph theory has applications in a wide range of fields, including computer networking, social network analysis, operations research, and cryptography.

Some of the key topics covered in graph theory include the following:

Graph terminology:
The basic terminology used in graphs, such as degree, path, cycle, and connectedness.

Graph representations:
There are different ways of representing graphs, such as adjacency lists and matrices.

Graph algorithms:
The algorithms are used for solving graph problems, such as traversal algorithms (breadth-first search, depth-first search) and shortest path algorithms (Dijkstra's algorithm).

Planar graphs:
Graphs that can be drawn on a plane without any edges crossing.

Graph colouring:

Assigning colours to vertices or edges of a graph is subject to certain constraints, such as ensuring that adjacent vertices or edges have different colours.

Graph theory applications:
Examples of real-world problems that can be modelled and solved using graph theory include scheduling and routing problems.

GRAPHS, VERTICES, AND EDGES

A graph is a mathematical structure consisting of vertices (also called nodes) and edges connecting these vertices. Vertices represent objects, and edges represent relationships or connections between these objects.

GRAPH REPRESENTATIONS

Graph representations are the methods of encoding graphs in a computer or a mathematical structure. Three popular representations of a graph are adjacency lists, adjacency matrices, and incidence matrices.

Adjacency list:
An adjacency list is a collection of unordered lists representing a finite graph. Each list describes the set of neighbours of a particular vertex in the graph. The advantage of using an adjacency list is that it allows for the efficient storage of sparse graphs.

Adjacency matrix:
An adjacency matrix is a square matrix used to represent a finite graph. The matrix contains one row and one column for each vertex in the graph, and the matrix entries represent the presence or absence of an edge between the corresponding vertices. The advantage of using an adjacency matrix is that it allows for efficient computation of certain graph properties, such as connectivity and shortest paths.

Introduction to Mathematics for Computing

Incidence matrix:

An incidence matrix is a rectangular matrix used to represent a finite graph. The matrix contains one row for each vertex and one column for each edge in the graph. The matrix entries represent whether or not a particular vertex is incident to a particular edge. The advantage of using an incidence matrix is that it allows for efficient computation of certain graph properties, such as the degree sequence of the graph.

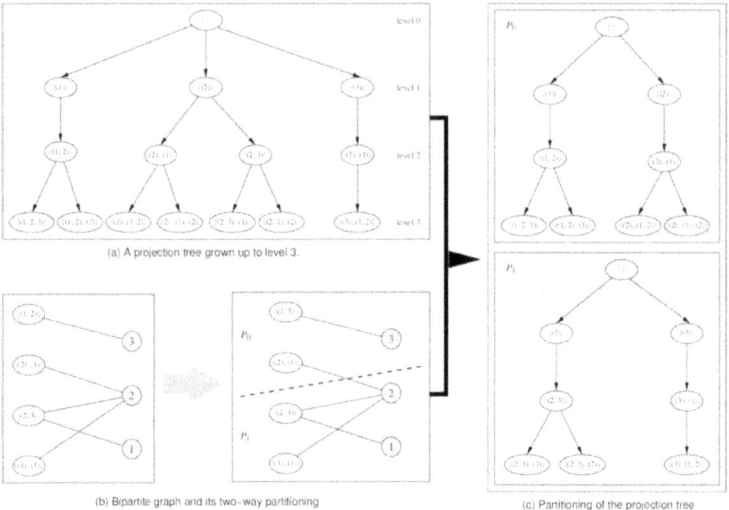

Figure 6 - An example of the bipartite graph-partitioning-based approach for task decomposition on two processors

The representation choice depends on the problem at hand and the graph's properties.

TYPES OF GRAPHS

Complete Graphs:
A complete graph is a graph where an edge connects every pair of vertices. In other words, the graph has an edge between every pair of vertices.

Bipartite Graphs:

A bipartite graph is a graph whose vertices can be partitioned into two disjoint sets such that every edge connects a vertex from one set to a vertex in the other set.

Trees:

In mathematics and computer science, a tree is a widely used abstract data type (ADT) that simulates a hierarchical tree structure with a set of linked nodes.

Properties of Trees:

- A tree is a connected acyclic graph.
- A tree with n nodes has n-1 edges.
- In a rooted tree, one node is designated as the root node, and all other nodes are descendants of the root node.
- Each node in a tree has a unique parent (except for the root node), and zero or more children.
- A node with no children is called a leaf node, and a node with at least one child is called an internal node.

Types of Trees:

- Binary Trees: A binary tree is a tree data structure in which each node has at most two children, referred to as the left and right child.
- Binary Search Trees: A binary search tree is a binary tree in which the value of each node is greater than or equal to the values in its left subtree and less than or equal to the values in its right subtree.
- AVL Trees: An AVL tree is a binary search tree in which the heights of every node's left and right subtrees differ by at least one. AVL stands for Adelson-Velskii and Landis, named after the

inventors G.M. Adelson-Velskii and E.M. Landis. It is a self-balancing binary search tree, where the height of the two subtrees of any node differs by at most one. AVL trees are commonly used in computer science due to their efficient operations on a sorted data set.
- B-Trees: A B-tree is a self-balancing search tree where each node can have multiple children, typically used in databases and file systems.

Operations on Trees:

- Traversals: The process of visiting each node in a tree exactly once is called a tree traversal. There are three types of traversals: inorder, preorder, and postorder.
- Insertion: The process of adding a new node to a tree is called insertion. The node is inserted in a binary search tree based on its value.
- Deletion: Removing a node from a tree is called a deletion. There are three cases for deletion: the node has no children, the node has one child, or the node has two children.
- Searching: Finding a particular node in a tree is called searching. In a binary search tree, the search is performed by comparing the value of the node with the target value and traversing the left or right subtree accordingly.

Planar Graphs:

A planar graph is a graph that can be drawn in such a way that no two edges cross each other.

There are many other types of graphs as well, such as directed graphs, weighted graphs, and multigraphs.

GRAPH REPRESENTATIONS

Adjacency Lists:

An adjacency list is a collection of unordered lists used to represent a finite graph. Each list describes the set of neighbours of a vertex in the graph.

Adjacency Matrices:

An adjacency matrix is a square matrix used to represent a finite graph. The elements of the matrix indicate whether pairs of vertices are adjacent or not.

Incidence Matrices:

An incidence matrix is a matrix that shows the relationship between the edges and vertices of a graph. Each row corresponds to an edge, and each column corresponds to a vertex. The element in the ith row and jth column is 1 if the edge i is incident to the vertex j, and 0 otherwise.

GRAPH PROPERTIES

Graphs have several properties:

Degree: The number of edges incident to a vertex.
Connectivity: A measure of the graph's robustness, indicating how difficult it is to disconnect the graph by removing vertices or edges.
Cycles: A sequence of vertices and edges that starts and ends at the same vertex.

GRAPH ALGORITHMS

Graph algorithms are a set of procedures that can be used to manipulate and analyse graphs. Here are some of the most common graph algorithms:

Breadth-first search (BFS):

BFS is a search algorithm that traverses a graph level by level, exploring all the nodes at one level before moving on to the next level. Imagine you have a network of friends on social media and want to find the shortest path from yourself to a particular friend. BFS can be used to search the network for the shortest path efficiently.

Depth-first search (DFS):

DFS is a search algorithm that explores as far as possible along each branch before backtracking. It can be implemented using either a stack or recursion. Consider a maze that needs to be solved. DFS can be used to explore all possible paths in the maze until the solution is found.

Dijkstra's algorithm:

The shortest path algorithm is used to find the shortest path between two nodes in a weighted graph. Imagine you have a weighted graph where the edges represent distances between locations, and you want to find the shortest path from one location to another. Dijkstra's algorithm can be used to find the shortest path efficiently.

Minimum spanning trees (MST):

MST is a set of edges that connect all the nodes in a graph while minimising the total cost of those edges. Suppose you have a set of cities and want to build a network of roads that connect them all while minimising the cost. Minimum spanning trees can be used to find the minimum cost network of roads that connects all the cities.

DISCRETE PROBABILITY

Discrete probability is a branch of mathematics that studies random events with a finite or countable number of possible outcomes. It plays a crucial role in computer science, particularly in algorithm analysis, cryptography, and artificial intelligence. This section will explore sample spaces and events, probability rules and axioms, conditional probability and independence, Bayes' theorem, and random variables and probability distributions.

SAMPLE SPACES AND EVENTS

A sample space is the set of all possible outcomes of a random experiment, typically denoted by the symbol Ω. An event is a subset of the sample space, representing a collection of outcomes that share a certain property.

PROBABILITY RULES AND AXIOMS

Probability is a measure that assigns a value between 0 and 1 to events, indicating the likelihood of the event occurring. The probability function P satisfies the following axioms:

Non-negativity: $P(A) \geq 0$ for any event A.
Normalisation: $P(\Omega) = 1$.
Countable additivity: If $A_1, A_2, \ldots$ are pairwise disjoint events (meaning no two events share any outcomes), then $P(\cup A_i) = \Sigma P(A_i)$.

CONDITIONAL PROBABILITY AND INDEPENDENCE

Conditional probability, denoted $P(A|B)$, is the probability of event A occurring, given that event B has occurred. Two events are considered independent if the occurrence of one does not affect the probability of the other. Mathematically, events A and B are independent if P(A ∩ B) = P(A)P(B).

Bayes' Theorem

Bayes' theorem is a fundamental result in probability theory, which relates the conditional probability of events. It states that for any two events A and B with P(B) ≠ 0:

$$P(A|B) = P(B|A)P(A) / P(B)$$

Bayes' theorem is extensively used in various fields, such as machine learning, artificial intelligence, and statistical inference.

Random Variables and Probability Distributions

A random variable is a function that assigns a real number to each outcome in a sample space. A probability distribution is a function that describes the probability of each possible value of a random variable.

Some common discrete probability distributions include:

Bernoulli distribution:
A random variable with only two possible outcomes, usually represented as success (1) and failure (0). The probability of success is p, and the probability of failure is 1 - p.

Binomial distribution:
A random variable representing the number of successes in n independent Bernoulli trials. The probability mass function is given by $P(X = k) = C(n, k)p^k(1 - p)^{(n - k)}$, where $C(n, k)$ is the number of combinations of n items taken k at a time.

Understanding discrete probability and its applications is essential for computer scientists and engineers in algorithm analysis, cryptography, and artificial intelligence.

RECURSION AND RECURRENCE RELATIONS

Recursion and recurrence relations are essential concepts in computer science and mathematics, particularly in the design and analysis of algorithms. Recursion refers to a problem-solving method where a function calls itself a subroutine to solve smaller instances of the same problem. Recurrence relations describe the relationship between the elements of a sequence based on a recursive formula. This section will explore recursive algorithms and functions, recurrence relations and their solutions, the master theorem, and generating functions for solving recurrences.

RECURSIVE ALGORITHMS AND FUNCTIONS

Recursive functions are functions that call themselves to perform a specific task. A recursive algorithm solves a problem by breaking it down into smaller subproblems, which are solved using the same algorithm. This approach is commonly used in computer programming, particularly in problems with a natural hierarchical or repetitive structure. An example of a recursive function is the calculation of the factorial of a number:

```lua
function factorial(n)
  if n <= 1 then
    return 1
  else
    return n * factorial(n-1)
  end if
end function
```

RECURRENCE RELATIONS AND THEIR SOLUTIONS

A recurrence relation is an equation that defines the terms of a sequence based on a recursive formula. For example, the Fibonacci sequence is defined by the recurrence relation F(n) = F(n-1) + F(n-2), with initial conditions F(0) = 0 and F(1) = 1. To find the solution of a recurrence relation, we can use methods such as substitution, iteration, or more advanced techniques like generating functions.

MASTER THEOREM FOR SOLVING RECURRENCES

A master theorem is a powerful tool for solving recurrence relations that arise in the analysis of divide-and-conquer algorithms. The theorem provides an asymptotic solution for recurrence relations of the form:

T(n) = aT(n/b) + f(n)

where $a \geq 1$, $b > 1$, and f(n) is an asymptotically positive function. The master theorem helps to determine the complexity of algorithms by providing a general solution to the recurrence relation, which can be expressed using big O notation.

GENERATING FUNCTIONS FOR SOLVING RECURRENCES

A generating function is a formal power series that encodes the information of a sequence. Generating functions can be used to find the closed-form solution of recurrence relations by manipulating the power series representation. By finding the closed-form expression of the generating function, we can extract the coefficients (which represent the terms of the sequence) and obtain a solution to the original recurrence relation.

Understanding recursion and recurrence relations is crucial for computer scientists and engineers, as these concepts play a significant role in the design and analysis of algorithms. For non-technical students, gaining familiarity with these ideas can provide valuable insight into problem-solving techniques and the underlying structure of various computational problems.

NUMBER THEORY

Number theory is a branch of mathematics that focuses on the properties and relationships of integers, especially positive integers or natural numbers. It is a foundational area of mathematics with cryptography, computer science, and more applications. This section will discuss divisibility and modular arithmetic, the Greatest Common Divisor (GCD) and Least Common Multiple (LCM), prime numbers and factorisation, Diophantine equations, and congruences and residues.

DIVISIBILITY AND MODULAR ARITHMETIC

Divisibility is the property of being divisible by another number without a remainder. For example, 15 is divisible by 3 because 15 = 3 × 5. Modular arithmetic, sometimes called "clock arithmetic," deals with the remainder when dividing numbers. It is denoted as "mod". For instance, 17 mod 5 = 2, because when we divide 17 by 5, the remainder is 2.

GCD AND LCM

The Greatest Common Divisor (GCD) of two integers is the largest positive integer that divides both numbers without a remainder. For example, the GCD of 18 and 12 is 6. The Least Common Multiple (LCM) of two integers is the smallest positive integer, a multiple of both numbers. For example, the LCM of 6 and 8 is 24.

PRIME NUMBERS AND FACTORISATION

A prime number is a natural number greater than 1 that has exactly two distinct factors: 1 and itself. Examples of prime numbers include 2, 3, 5, 7, and 11. The factorisation is the process of breaking down a number into its prime factors. For example, the prime factorisation of 28 is $2 \times 2 \times 7$ or $2^2 \times 7$.

DIOPHANTINE EQUATIONS

Diophantine equations are polynomial equations with integer coefficients where we seek integer solutions. For example, the Pythagorean equation $x^2 + y^2 = z^2$ is a Diophantine equation, and one solution is $x = 3$, $y = 4$, and $z = 5$.

CONGRUENCES AND RESIDUES

A congruence is an equation that expresses the equivalence of two numbers with respect to a given modulus. For example, $15 \equiv 2 \pmod{13}$ means that 15 and 2 have the same remainder when divided by 13. Residues are the possible remainders in modular arithmetic. For instance, residues modulo 4 are $\{0, 1, 2, 3\}$.

Finite Automata and Formal Languages

Finite automata and formal languages are crucial in studying computation and designing programming languages. These concepts help us understand how computers process information and accept valid input. This section will introduce deterministic finite automata (DFA), nondeterministic finite automata (NFA), regular expressions, context-free grammars, and pushdown automata.

Deterministic Finite Automata (DFA)

As previously mentioned, a deterministic finite automaton (DFA) is a theoretical model of computation that consists of a finite set of states, an input alphabet, a transition function, an initial state, and a set of accepting states. DFA recognises regular languages, and its deterministic property ensures that its behaviour is entirely predictable.

Nondeterministic Finite Automata (NFA)

Nondeterministic finite automata (NFA) are similar to DFA but allow multiple transitions for a given state and input symbol. This means an NFA can be in multiple states simultaneously, making its behaviour non-deterministic. NFAs are also used to recognise regular languages, and every NFA can be converted into an equivalent DFA.

Regular Expressions

Regular expressions are formal notations used to describe patterns in strings. They are closely related to finite automata, as both are used to recognise regular languages. Regular expressions can be used to search for specific patterns in text, validate user input, or manipulate strings in various ways. Examples of regular expressions include:

"a*b" matches any string that contains zero or more 'a's followed by a single 'b'.

"(ab|cd)" matches either the string 'ab' or the string 'cd'.

9.4. Context-Free Grammars

Context-free grammars (CFGs) are a more expressive formalism that describes languages that regular expressions or finite automata cannot recognise. CFGs are particularly useful for modelling the syntax of programming languages and natural languages. Context-free grammar consists of a set of production rules that describe how to generate strings in the language.

PUSHDOWN AUTOMATA

Pushdown automata (PDA) are an extension of finite automata that include a stack, a data structure that operates in a last-in, first-out (LIFO) manner. The stack allows pushdown automata to recognise context-free languages that are more complex than regular ones. PDAs have a finite set of states, an input alphabet, a stack alphabet, a transition function, an initial state, and a set of accepting states. The additional memory provided by the stack enables PDAs to recognise languages with nested structures, such as balanced parentheses or nested function calls.

These topics provide an overview of finite automata and formal languages, which are essential concepts for understanding the theoretical underpinnings of computer science and the design of programming languages.

ALGORITHMS AND DATA STRUCTURES

In computer science, algorithms and data structures are essential concepts that help solve problems efficiently. An algorithm is a step-by-step procedure to accomplish a task, while a data structure organises and stores data.

OVERVIEW OF ALGORITHMS AND THEIR CHARACTERISTICS

An algorithm is defined by its input, output, and the sequence of steps to transform the input into the desired output. Algorithms can have different characteristics, such as correctness, efficiency, and robustness. Choosing the right algorithm depends on the specific problem and constraints, such as time, memory, and available resources.

ALGORITHM COMPLEXITY AND BIG-O NOTATION

Algorithm complexity refers to the amount of resources (time and memory) an algorithm requires as a function of input size. Big-O notation describes the upper bound of an algorithm's complexity, which represents the worst-case scenario. For example, $O(n)$ represents linear complexity, where the algorithm's running time increases linearly with the input size.

DATA STRUCTURES USED IN COMPUTING

Data structures are used to store and manage data efficiently. Some common data structures are:

Arrays:
A fixed-size collection of elements of the same data type, stored in contiguous memory locations.

Linked Lists: A collection of elements, called nodes, where each node points to the next node in the sequence.

Stacks: A collection of elements with Last-In-First-Out (LIFO) access, where elements are added and removed from the top of the stack.

Queues:
A collection of elements with First-In-First-Out (FIFO) access, where elements are added at the rear and removed from the front.

Trees:
A hierarchical data structure consisting of nodes connected by edges, with a single root node and no cycles.

Graphs:
A collection of nodes and edges that can represent relationships between objects.

SEARCHING ALGORITHMS

Searching algorithms are used to find a particular element in a data structure. Two common searching algorithms are:

***Linear search*:**
A simple search algorithm that iterates through each element in a list until the target element is found. In the worst case, the time complexity is O(n).

Binary search:
A more efficient search algorithm that works on sorted lists. It repeatedly divides the list in half until the target element is found or the search interval is empty. The worst-case time complexity is O(log n).

SORTING ALGORITHMS

Sorting algorithms arrange elements in a particular order, such as ascending or descending. Some common sorting algorithms are:

Bubble sort:
A simple sorting algorithm that repeatedly steps through the list, compares adjacent elements, and swaps them if they are in the wrong order. The worst-case time complexity is $O(n^2)$.

Insertion sort:
A sorting algorithm that builds the final sorted array one element at a time. It is much less efficient on large lists than other algorithms like merge sort or quick sort. The worst-case time complexity is $O(n^2)$.

Merge sort:
A divide-and-conquer sorting algorithm that works by dividing the list into two halves, recursively sorting each half, and then merging the two sorted halves. The worst-case time complexity is $O(n \log n)$.

Quick sort:
Another divide-and-conquer sorting algorithm that works by selecting a 'pivot' element from the array and partitioning the other elements into two groups, those less than the pivot and those greater than the pivot. The worst-case time complexity is $O(n^2)$, but in practice, quick sort is often faster than other sorting algorithms.

These topics provide an overview of algorithms and data structures, essential concepts for understanding computer science fundamentals and problem-solving.

Chapter 2 Exercises and More

Below you will find a set of practice questions and their corresponding answers. In addition, this section includes key takeaways from the chapter to help reinforce your understanding of the material.

Practice Questions

1. Given sets A = {1, 2, 3} and B = {2, 3, 4}, find the union (A ∪ B), intersection (A ∩ B), and difference (A - B) of the two sets.
2. Construct a truth table for the following logical expression: (P ∧ Q) → (¬P ∨ R).
3. How many unique ways can you arrange the letters of the word "COMPUTE"? Assume all letters are distinct.
4. In a group of 20 people, there are 8 people who like tea, 10 people who like coffee, and 4 people who like both. Using the Inclusion-Exclusion Principle, how many people in the group like either tea or coffee?
5. Given the graph G with vertices A, B, C, D, and E and the following edges: {A, B}, {A, C}, {B, C}, {B, D}, {C, E}. Represent this graph using an adjacency matrix and an adjacency list.
6. A fair six-sided die is rolled twice. What is the probability of obtaining a sum of 7 from the two rolls?
7. Solve the following linear recurrence relation: $T(n) = 3T(n-1) + 5$, with $T(0) = 1$.
8. Determine the greatest common divisor (GCD) of 56 and 98 using the Euclidean algorithm.
9. Given the deterministic finite automaton (DFA) with states {q_0, q_1, q_2} and the following transition rules: (q_0, 0) → q_1, (q_0, 1) → q_0, (q_1, 0) → q_1, (q_1, 1) → q_2, (q_2, 0) → q_2, (q_2, 1) → q_0. Determine whether the input string "010101" is accepted by the DFA.

10. Consider an array of integers: [5, 3, 7, 1, 8, 2]. Apply the first two iterations of the bubble sort algorithm on the array and write down the intermediate arrays after each iteration.

KEY TAKEAWAYS

- Set theory is a foundational concept in discrete mathematics, dealing with collections of distinct objects and the various operations that can be performed on these collections, such as union, intersection, difference, and complement.
- Propositional logic and propositional calculus form the basis of logical reasoning in mathematics and computer science. They involve propositions, logical connectives, truth tables, logical equivalence, and proof techniques.
- Combinatorics deals with counting and arranging objects in various ways, including permutations, combinations, the pigeonhole principle, and binomial coefficients.
- Graph theory studies mathematical structures used to model pairwise relations between objects. It covers various types of graphs, their properties, representations, and algorithms.
- Discrete probability is a branch of probability that deals with discrete sample spaces and events. It covers probability rules, conditional probability, independence, Bayes' theorem, and random variables with probability distributions.
- Recursion and recurrence relations define functions or solve problems that depend on previous values. They are crucial for designing algorithms and understanding their time complexity.
- Number theory studies the properties and relationships of integers, involving concepts like divisibility, modular arithmetic, prime numbers, and Diophantine equations.
- Finite automata and formal languages are used to model and analyse the behaviour of simple computational systems. They include deterministic and nondeterministic finite automata, regular expressions, and pushdown automata.

- Algorithms and data structures are fundamental concepts in computer science that help solve problems efficiently. They involve understanding algorithm complexity, big-O notation, various data structures, and searching and sorting algorithms.

LIST OF SYMBOLS FROM CHAPTER 2

Here is a list of symbols used in Chapter 2:

- ∈ (element of): A symbol used to denote that an element is a member of a set.
- ⊆ (subset): A symbol used to represent that one set is a subset of another set.
- ⊂ (proper subset): A symbol used to represent that one set is a proper subset of another set.
- ∪ (union): A symbol used to denote the union of two sets.
- ∩ (intersection): A symbol used to denote the intersection of two sets.
- \ (difference): A symbol used to denote the difference between two sets.
- ⁻ (complement): A symbol used to denote the complement of a set.
- × (Cartesian product): A symbol used to denote the Cartesian product of two sets.
- ↔ (biconditional): A symbol used to represent logical equivalence or "if and only if" in propositional logic.
- → (implication): A symbol used to represent logical implication or "if-then" in propositional logic.
- ¬ (negation): A symbol used to represent the logical negation of a proposition.
- ∧ (conjunction): A symbol used to represent the logical AND of two propositions.

Introduction to Mathematics for Computing

- ∨ (disjunction): A symbol used to represent the logical OR of two propositions.
- ∀ (universal quantifier): A symbol used to represent "for all" in predicate logic.
- ∃ (existential quantifier): A symbol used to represent "there exists" in predicate logic.
- ≡ (congruent): A symbol used to denote congruence in modular arithmetic.
- | (divides): A symbol used to denote that one integer divides another integer without leaving a remainder.
- gcd (greatest common divisor): A notation used to represent the greatest common divisor of two integers.
- lcm (least common multiple): A notation used to represent the least common multiple of two integers.

ANSWERS TO THE PRACTICE QUESTIONS

1. $A \cup B = \{1, 2, 3, 4\}$, $A \cap B = \{2, 3\}$, $A - B = \{1\}$
2. The truth table for the expression $(P \wedge Q) \rightarrow (\neg P \vee R)$ is as follows:

P	Q	R	¬P	P∧Q	¬P∨R	(P∧Q) → (¬P∨R)
T	T	T	F	T	T	T
T	T	F	F	T	F	F
T	F	T	F	F	T	T
T	F	F	F	F	F	T
F	T	T	T	F	T	T
F	T	F	T	F	T	T
F	F	T	T	F	T	T
F	F	F	T	F	T	T

3. There are $7! = 5{,}040$ unique ways to arrange the letters of the word "COMPUTE".
4. Using the Inclusion-Exclusion Principle, the number of people who like either tea or coffee is $8 + 10 - 4 = 14$.
5. Adjacency matrix representation:

    A B C D E

```
A 0 1 1 0 0
B 1 0 1 1 0
C 1 1 0 0 1
D 0 1 0 0 0
E 0 0 1 0 0
```

Adjacency list representation:

A: [B, C]
B: [A, C, D]
C: [A, B, E]
D: [B]
E: [C]

6. The probability of obtaining a sum of 7 from two rolls of a fair six-sided die is 6/36 = 1/6.
7. The solution to the linear recurrence relation $T(n) = 3T(n-1) + 5$, with $T(0) = 1$, is $T(n) = 2(3^n) - 1$.
8. The GCD(56, 98) is 14.
9. The input string "010101" is accepted by the given DFA, as it ends in state q2.
10. Applying the first two iterations of the bubble sort algorithm on the array [5, 3, 7, 1, 8, 2]:
    1st iteration: [3, 5, 1, 7, 2, 8]
    2nd iteration: [3, 1, 5, 2, 7, 8]

CHAPTER 3

LINEAR ALGEBRA AND CALCULUS

This chapter will explore two fundamental branches of mathematics, Linear Algebra and Calculus. Despite their seemingly complex nature, these mathematical disciplines provide essential tools for solving real-world problems and understanding the world around us. Both subjects significantly impact various fields, including computer science, engineering, physics, and more.

Linear Algebra is the study of vector spaces and linear transformations between them. It focuses on the properties and relationships of vectors, matrices, and systems of linear equations. It forms the foundation for many computer algorithms, including those used in graphics, data analysis, and machine learning. For example, when managing a network of computers, Linear Algebra can help optimise data flow and resource allocation.

Conversely, calculus is a branch of mathematics concerned with the study of change and motion. It allows us to understand and predict the behaviour of continuously changing quantities. For instance, Calculus can be used to determine the trajectory of a projectile or model the spread of disease. Calculus is divided into two main branches: Differential Calculus, which deals with rates of change, and Integral Calculus, which focuses on accumulation and area. These concepts are fundamental in various fields, including physics, engineering, and economics.

Throughout this chapter, we will delve into the key aspects of both Linear Algebra and Calculus, offering non-CSE students a solid foundation in these essential mathematical subjects. We will provide practical examples that demonstrate how these mathematical concepts can be applied in various real-life situations and within the field of computer science. By the end of this chapter, you will better understand the importance and applications of Linear Algebra and Calculus.

LINER ALGEBRA

Algebra is a branch of mathematics that deals with mathematical symbols and the rules for manipulating these symbols. The word "algebra" comes from the Arabic word "al-jabr," which means "reunion of broken parts." This term was introduced by the Persian mathematician Al-Khwarizmi in his book "Kitab al-mukhtasar fi hisab al-jabr wa'l-muqabala," which translates to "The Compendious Book on Calculation by Completion and Balancing." Written in the 9th century, this book provided a systematic approach to solving linear and quadratic equations, laying the foundation for the development of algebra as we know it today.

The introduction of algebra marked a significant shift from the earlier arithmetic-based methods, as it allowed for more abstract and symbolic representation of mathematical problems. This paved the way for further advancements in mathematics, including the development of Linear Algebra, which we will explore in this chapter. As we dive into Linear Algebra and Calculus, it's essential to appreciate the historical context and the origins of algebra, which have shaped the mathematical landscape and facilitated the study of these topics for non-CSE students.

Linear Algebra is a branch of mathematics that studies vector spaces, linear transformations, and systems of linear equations. It emerged in the early 19th century as a result of the efforts of mathematicians like Augustin-Louis Cauchy, William Rowan Hamilton, and Arthur Cayley, who sought to generalise the methods of solving linear equations to more abstract settings. Linear Algebra has since become an essential tool in various fields, including computer science, engineering, and physics.

At its core, Linear Algebra focuses on manipulating vectors and matrices to solve problems. Vectors are mathematical objects that represent both magnitude and direction, while matrices are rectangular arrays of numbers, symbols, or expressions. By working with these structures, Linear Algebra allows us to model and solve complex problems more streamlined and efficient. Let's understand this closely with some examples:

Example 1:
Suppose we want to find the profit made by a shop that sells three different items. The shopkeeper knows the price of each item and the number of items sold. We can use Linear Algebra to represent the price of items as a vector and the number of items sold as another vector. We can quickly compute the total profit by performing a dot product between these two vectors.

Example 2:
Linear Algebra plays a crucial role in transforming and manipulating graphical objects in computer graphics. For example, matrices represent these transformations when a video game character moves or rotates. By multiplying the original coordinates of the character with a transformation matrix, we can obtain the new position and orientation of the character in the game world.

Example 3:
Linear Algebra is used in data analysis to perform operations on large datasets. For instance, when working with a dataset that contains information about multiple variables, such as age, income, and education level, we can represent this data as a matrix. Linear Algebra techniques, like matrix multiplication and inversion, can then be employed to extract meaningful insights, such as finding correlations between variables or predicting future trends.

These examples illustrate the versatility and practicality of Linear Algebra in various fields and applications, making it an essential subject for non-CSE students to grasp.

In this section, we will delve into the fascinating world of Linear Algebra, which is a branch of mathematics that deals with linear equations, linear transformations, and their representations using matrices and vector spaces. Linear Algebra has numerous applications in various fields, including computer science, physics, engineering, and data science. We will explore some fundamental concepts and operations in Linear Algebra, which will serve as building blocks for understanding more advanced topics. By the end of this section, you will have a solid foundation in the basics of Linear Algebra, and you will be able to grasp the ideas and methods that underpin many of the algorithms and techniques used in computing and data analysis. The topics we will cover in this section are as follows:

SCALARS, VECTORS, AND MATRICES

Scalars are single numerical values, whereas vectors are ordered lists of numbers. Matrices are rectangular arrays of numbers arranged in rows and columns. Example: scalar - 5, vector - [2, 4, 6], matrix - [[1, 2], [3, 4], [5, 6]].

MATRIX OPERATIONS

Addition: Adding two matrices of the same dimensions by adding corresponding elements. Example: [[1, 2], [3, 4]] + [[5, 6], [7, 8]] = [[6, 8], [10, 12]].

Subtraction: Subtracting two matrices of the same dimensions by subtracting corresponding elements. Example: [[6, 8], [10, 12]] - [[1, 2], [3, 4]] = [[5, 6], [7, 8]].

Multiplication: Multiplying two matrices with compatible dimensions (number of columns in the first matrix equals the number of rows in the second matrix) by taking the dot product of rows and columns. Example: [[1, 2], [3, 4]] × [[5, 6], [7, 8]] = [[19, 22], [43, 50]].

Scalar multiplication: Multiplying a matrix by a scalar by multiplying each element by the scalar. Example: 2 × [[1, 2], [3, 4]] = [[2, 4], [6, 8]].

TRANSPOSE OF A MATRIX

The transpose of a matrix is obtained by exchanging its rows and columns. Example: Transpose of [[1, 2], [3, 4], [5, 6]] is [[1, 3, 5], [2, 4, 6]].

IDENTITY AND INVERSE MATRICES

The identity matrix is a square matrix with 1s along the diagonal and 0s elsewhere. Example: 2x2 identity matrix - [[1, 0], [0, 1]]. The inverse of a square matrix A is another matrix, denoted as $A^{(-1)}$, such that their product equals the identity matrix. Example: A = [[2, 1], [5, 3]], $A^{(-1)}$ = [[3, -1], [-5, 2]], A × $A^{(-1)}$ = [[1, 0], [0, 1]].

SYSTEMS OF LINEAR EQUATIONS AND GAUSSIAN ELIMINATION

A system of linear equations is a collection of equations involving variables that need to be solved simultaneously. Using row operations, gaussian elimination solves these systems by transforming the augmented matrix into its reduced row echelon form. Example: Solve the system {x + y = 3, 2x - y = 1} using Gaussian elimination.

RANK OF A MATRIX

The rank of a matrix is the number of linearly independent rows or columns it has. Example: The rank of the matrix [[1, 2], [2, 4]] is 1, as the second row is a multiple of the first row.

DETERMINANTS AND THEIR PROPERTIES

The determinant is a scalar value that can be computed for square matrices and has several important properties. It is a measure of the scaling factor when transforming a vector space. Example: The determinant of a 2x2 matrix [[a, b], [c, d]] is ad - bc.

Cramer's Rule for Solving Linear Systems

Cramer's rule is a method for solving linear systems using determinants. It states that if the determinant of the coefficient matrix is nonzero, the system has a unique solution, given by the quotient of the determinant of a modified coefficient matrix and the determinant of the original coefficient matrix. Example: Solve the system {x + y = 3, 2x - y = 1} using Cramer's rule.

Vector Spaces and Their Properties

A vector space is a set of vectors that is closed under vector addition and scalar multiplication and satisfies several axioms (associativity, commutativity, existence of identity and inverse elements, and distributive properties). Example: The set of all 2-dimensional vectors, R^2, is a vector space.

Subspaces and Bases

A subspace is a subset of a vector space that is also a vector space under the same operations. A basis is a set of linearly independent vectors that span a vector space. Example: The set {[(1, 0), (0, 1)]} is a basis for R^2.

Linear Transformations and Their Properties

A linear transformation is a function that maps vectors from one vector space to another, preserving the operations of vector addition and scalar multiplication. Example: The function T(x, y) = (2x, 3y) is a linear transformation from R^2 to R^2.

Kernel and Image of a Linear Transformation

The kernel of a linear transformation is the set of all vectors that map to the zero vector. The image is the set of all vectors that can be obtained as the output of the transformation. Example: For the linear transformation T(x, y) = (x - y, 0), the kernel is the set of all vectors (x, y) such that x = y, and the image is the set of all vectors (x, 0).

EIGENVECTORS AND EIGENVALUES

Eigenvectors are non-zero vectors that remain parallel to themselves after a linear transformation. Eigenvalues are the scalar factors by which the eigenvectors are stretched or compressed. Example: For the matrix [[2, 1], [1, 2]], eigenvectors are (1, 1) and (1, -1), and the corresponding eigenvalues are 3 and 1, respectively.

DIAGONALISATION OF A MATRIX

Diagonalisation is the process of finding an invertible matrix P and a diagonal matrix D such that $A = PDP^{-1}$, where A is a given square matrix. The diagonal entries of D are the eigenvalues of A, and the columns of P are the corresponding eigenvectors. Example: Diagonalise the matrix [[2, 1], [1, 2]].

ORTHOGONALITY AND GRAM-SCHMIDT PROCESS

The Gram-Schmidt process is a method for constructing an orthogonal basis for a given subspace. Orthogonality is a property in which two vectors are perpendicular to each other, meaning their dot product is zero. Example: Apply the Gram-Schmidt process to the vectors (1, 1) and (1, -1) in R^2.

CALCULUS

Calculus is a branch of mathematics that deals with the study of change, motion, and accumulation. It was developed independently by two mathematicians, Sir Isaac Newton and Gottfried Wilhelm Leibniz, in the late 17th century. Calculus is crucial in numerous fields, such as physics, engineering, economics, and computer science. It enables us to model real-world phenomena by providing tools to understand and analyse the relationships between variables.

It provides a systematic framework for analysing and understanding continuous processes and functions characterised by variables that change smoothly over a range of values. Calculus is divided into two main branches: differential calculus and integral calculus.

Differential calculus deals with the concept of the derivative, which measures the rate at which a function changes concerning its independent variable. It helps us understand how a quantity changes concerning another, allowing us to predict and analyse the behaviour of dynamic systems.

Integral calculus, however, deals with the integral concept, which measures the accumulation of a quantity over a given interval. It helps us calculate areas, volumes, and other accumulated values and determine the total effect of a continuously changing variable. Let us look at some examples:

Example 1:
In physics, calculus determines moving objects' position, velocity, and acceleration. For instance, if we know the acceleration of an object, we can use calculus to find its velocity and position at any given time.

Example 2:
Economics employs calculus to find the optimal production levels and business pricing strategies. Companies can make informed

decisions about their operations by examining how profit changes with respect to the number of products produced or the price charged.

Example 3:

In computer graphics, calculus models the smooth surfaces and curves in 3D objects. By understanding how the curvature of surface changes, we can create realistic and visually appealing images and animations.

In this section, we will introduce the fundamental concepts of calculus, which will equip you with the knowledge needed to tackle various real-world problems. Let's deep dive:

D̲ifferential C̲alculus

Differential calculus is a branch of calculus that focuses on studying the rates of change of functions concerning their input variables. The primary concept in differential calculus is derivative, which represents a function's instantaneous rate of change at a particular point. The process of finding the derivative of a function is called differentiation. Differential calculus is used in various fields, such as physics, engineering, and economics, to model and solve problems involving rates of change, velocities, and slopes of curves.

I̲ntegral C̲alculus:

Integral calculus is the complementary branch of calculus that deals with accumulating quantities over an interval. It focuses on finding the area under a curve, the total accumulated change, or the total quantity accumulated over a given range. The primary concept in integral calculus is integral, which represents the accumulated change of a function over an interval. The process of finding the integral of a function is called integration. Integral calculus is widely used in different disciplines, including physics, engineering, and economics, to calculate areas, volumes, and accumulated quantities and solve problems involving continuous change or accumulation.

FUNCTIONS AND THEIR GRAPHS

A function is a mathematical relationship between two sets of numbers, where each input (also known as an independent variable) has exactly one corresponding output (dependent variable). Functions are commonly denoted as f(x), where x is the input and f(x) is the output. Graphs of functions visually represent the relationship between the input and output values.

Example: The function f(x) = x^2 represents a quadratic function. Plotting the points on a graph allows us to visualise the relationship between the input x and the output f(x).

LIMITS AND CONTINUITY

A limit is a fundamental concept in calculus that describes the behaviour of a function as the input approaches a specific value. It is denoted as lim(x→a) f(x) = L, which means that as x gets closer to 'a', the function f(x) gets arbitrarily close to L.

Example: The limit of the function f(x) = (x^2 - 1)/(x - 1) as x approaches 1 is 2, even though the function is not defined at x = 1.

LIMIT LAWS

Limit laws are rules that allow us to manipulate and simplify limits algebraically. These rules include sum, difference, product, and quotient laws.

Example: Given the limits lim(x→a) g(x) = M and lim(x→a) h(x) = N, the limit of the sum of the functions is lim(x→a) [g(x) + h(x)] = M + N.

CONTINUITY

A function is continuous at a point if the limit exists at that point and the function's value is equal to the limit. In other words, a function is continuous if there are no abrupt changes or jumps in its values as the input varies.

Example: The function $f(x) = x^2$ is continuous for all real numbers x, as there are no abrupt changes or gaps in the graph of the function.

DEFINITION OF DERIVATIVE

The derivative of a function measures the rate at which the function is changing with respect to the input. It is denoted as $f'(x)$ or $df(x)/dx$ and represents the slope of the tangent line to the graph of the function at a given point.

Example: The derivative of the function $f(x) = x^2$ is $f'(x) = 2x$.

RULES FOR DIFFERENTIATION

Differentiation rules are techniques for finding derivatives of functions, such as the power rule, product rule, quotient rule, and chain rule.

Example: Using the power rule, the derivative of the function $f(x) = x^n$, where n is a constant, is $f'(x) = nx^{(n-1)}$.

APPLICATIONS OF DERIVATIVES

Derivatives have various applications, such as determining the rate of change, finding maximum and minimum values of functions, and solving optimisation problems.

Example: The derivative of the position function, s(t), gives the velocity function, v(t), which describes how the position of an object changes over time.

HIGHER-ORDER DERIVATIVES

Higher-order derivatives are derivatives of derivatives. The second derivative, denoted as f''(x), represents the rate of change of the first derivative, and so on for higher orders. These higher-order derivatives can be used to analyse the curvature and concavity of a function's graph.

Example: The second derivative of the function $f(x) = x^3$ is $f''(x) = 6x$, which describes the rate of change of the function's slope.

INTEGRATION

Integration is the reverse process of differentiation, allowing us to find the area under a curve or accumulate quantities over a given interval. Integrals are denoted using the integral symbol ∫ and can be classified as definite integrals (with specific interval limits) or indefinite integrals (without specific limits).

Example: The integral of the function $f(x) = x^2$ is $\int x^2 \, dx$.

RULES FOR INTEGRATION

Integration rules are techniques for finding integrals of functions, such as the power rule for integration, substitution method, integration by parts, and partial fractions.

Example: Using the power rule for integration, the indefinite integral of the function $f(x) = x^n$, where $n \neq -1$, is $\int x^n \, dx = x^{(n+1)}/(n+1) + C$, where C is the constant of integration.

APPLICATIONS OF INTEGRALS

Integrals have various applications, such as calculating areas, volumes, and accumulated quantities in different fields, including physics, engineering, and economics.

Example: To find the area under the curve of the function $f(x) = x^2$ between the points $x = 1$ and $x = 3$, we evaluate the definite integral $\int_1^3 x^2 \, dx$.

DIFFERENTIAL EQUATIONS

A differential equation is an equation that relates a function and its derivatives. Differential equations are used to model various phenomena in fields like physics, biology, and finance. They can be classified as ordinary differential equations (involving one independent variable) or partial differential equations (involving multiple independent variables).

Example: Newton's law of cooling is a first-order ordinary differential equation that describes how the temperature of an object changes over time.

CHAPTER 3 EXERCISES AND MORE

Below, you will find a set of practice questions and their corresponding answers. In addition, this section includes key takeaways and symbols from the chapter to help reinforce your understanding of the material.

PRACTICE QUESTIONS

1. What is the difference between a scalar and a vector? Provide an example of each.
2. Define the dot product and cross product of two vectors, and explain how to compute each operation.
3. What are the three elementary row operations that can be performed on a matrix? Describe a situation where each operation might be useful.
4. How do you determine if a system of linear equations has a unique solution, infinitely many solutions, or no solution?
5. Explain the concept of a determinant, and describe how to calculate the determinant of a 2x2 and 3x3 matrix.
6. What is the difference between a basis and a span of a vector space? Provide an example to illustrate your answer.
7. Describe the process of finding eigenvectors and eigenvalues of a square matrix. How are they useful in linear algebra applications?
8. Define the limit of a function and explain its significance in calculus. Provide an example of a function with a limit at a particular point.
9. Differentiate the function $f(x) = x^3 + 2x^2 - 3x + 1$ with respect to x, and find the critical points of the function.
10. Evaluate the definite integral of the function $g(x) = 2x^2 - 4x + 3$ over the interval [0, 2]. Explain the result's significance in the context of the area under the curve.

KEY TAKEAWAYS

- Linear algebra is a branch of mathematics that deals with vectors, vector spaces, linear transformations, and matrices, while calculus focuses on the study of change and motion through limits, derivatives, and integrals.
- Vectors are ordered lists of numbers that can be added, subtracted, and scaled. They can represent quantities such as position, velocity, and force in physics and engineering.
- Matrices are rectangular arrays of numbers representing linear transformations and systems of linear equations. They can be added, subtracted, and multiplied using specific rules.
- Systems of linear equations can be solved using methods like Gaussian elimination, which involves elementary row operations to transform the matrix into a simpler form.
- Determinants are scalar values calculated for square matrices and are used to find the inverse of a matrix, check if a matrix is singular, and determine the volume scaling factor of a linear transformation.
- Vector spaces and linear transformations are fundamental concepts in linear algebra. A vector space is a set of vectors closed under addition and scalar multiplication, while a linear transformation is a function that preserves vector addition and scalar multiplication.
- Eigenvectors and eigenvalues are properties of square matrices that reveal important information about the matrix, such as the directions in which a linear transformation stretches or compresses space.
- Calculus is divided into two main branches: differential calculus, which focuses on the rates of change and slopes of curves through derivatives, and integral calculus, which deals with the accumulation of quantities and areas under curves through integrals.

- The limit of a function is the value that the function approaches as the input gets arbitrarily close to a specific point, which allows us to study the behaviour of functions near points of discontinuity or undefined values.
- Derivatives and integrals have numerous applications in various fields, including physics, engineering, economics, and biology. They are used to model and solve problems involving rates of change, optimisation, motion, and areas under curves.

SYMBOLS USED IN THIS CHAPTER

Here's a list of symbols commonly used in Chapter 3, covering Linear Algebra and Calculus:

- $\mathbb{R}$: Set of real numbers
- $A, B, C, \ldots$: Matrices
- $a_{ij}, b_{ij}, c_{ij}, \ldots$: Matrix elements
- $n \times m$: Matrix dimensions (n rows and m columns)
- I: Identity matrix
- A^{-1}: Inverse of matrix A
- A^T: Transpose of matrix A
- $\mathbf{x}, \mathbf{y}, \mathbf{z}, \ldots$: Vectors
- $x_1, x_2, x_3, \ldots$: Vector components
- $|\mathbf{x}|$: Magnitude of vector $\mathbf{x}$
- $\langle \mathbf{x}, \mathbf{y} \rangle$: Inner product (dot product) of vectors $\mathbf{x}$ and $\mathbf{y}$
- $f(x)$: A function of variable x
- $f'(x), f''(x), \ldots$: First, second, ... derivatives of $f(x)$
- dy/dx: Derivative of y with respect to x
- $\int f(x)dx$: Indefinite integral of $f(x)$ with respect to x
- $\int(a, b) f(x)dx$: Definite integral of $f(x)$ with respect to x over the interval $[a, b]$
- $\lim (x \to a) f(x)$: Limit of $f(x)$ as x approaches a
- Σ: Summation symbol
- Π: Product Symbol

These are some of the most common symbols used in Linear Algebra and Calculus. You may encounter additional symbols depending on the specific topics covered in the chapter.

ANSWERS TO THE PRACTICE QUESTIONS

- A scalar is a single numerical value, while a vector is an ordered list of numbers. For example, a scalar could be the number 5, while a vector could be (2, 3).
- The dot product of two vectors is the sum of the products of their corresponding components, while the cross product is a vector orthogonal to both input vectors. Dot product: $A \cdot B = \Sigma(A_i * B_i)$. Cross product (for 3D vectors): $A \times B = (A_yB_z - A_zB_y, A_zB_x - A_xB_z, A_xB_y - A_yB_x)$.
- The three elementary row operations are: (a) swapping two rows, (b) multiplying a row by a non-zero scalar, and (c) adding or subtracting a multiple of one row to another row. These operations are useful for solving systems of linear equations and finding the inverse of a matrix.
- A system of linear equations has a unique solution if the matrix has full rank, infinitely many solutions if the matrix has less than full rank and the system is consistent, and no solution if the system is inconsistent.
- A determinant is a scalar value calculated for square matrices, which provides information about the matrix's properties. For a 2x2 matrix: $det(A) = ad - bc$. For a 3x3 matrix: $det(A) = a(ei - fh) - b(di - fg) + c(dh - eg)$.
- A basis is a set of linearly independent vectors that spans the entire vector space, whereas the span is the set of all linear combinations of a given set of vectors. For example, {(1, 0), (0, 1)} is a basis for R^2, and the span of {(2, 1), (1, 2)} is R^2.
- To find the eigenvectors and eigenvalues of a square matrix A, first find the characteristic equation, which is $det(A - \lambda I) = 0$, where λ is the eigenvalue and I is the identity matrix. Solve the

equation for λ to find the eigenvalues. Then, for each eigenvalue, solve the equation $(A - \lambda I)v = 0$ for the eigenvector v.
- The limit of a function f(x) as x approaches a point c is the value that f(x) approaches as x gets arbitrarily close to c. For example, the limit of the function $f(x) = (x^2 - 1)/(x - 1)$ as x approaches 1 is 2, since f(x) approaches 2 as x gets close to 1.
- The derivative of $f(x) = x^3 + 2x^2 - 3x + 1$ with respect to x is $f'(x) = 3x^2 + 4x - 3$. To find the critical points, set $f'(x) = 0$ and solve for x. The critical points are $x = 1$ and $x = -1$.
- To evaluate the definite integral of $g(x) = 2x^2 - 4x + 3$ over the interval [0, 2], find the antiderivative $G(x) = (2/3)x^3 - 2x^2 + 3x$ and then compute $G(2) - G(0)$. The result is 2/3. The significance of the result is that it represents the net signed area under the curve of g(x) from $x = 0$ to $x = 2$.

CHAPTER 4

PROBABILITY AND STATISTICS

Probability and statistics are two closely linked branches of mathematics that focus on understanding and managing uncertainty and organising and analysing data. They often work hand in hand, providing a comprehensive framework for making predictions, informed decisions, and generalisations about complex situations.

Probability is the mathematical study of chance and likelihood. It deals with the quantification of uncertainty and the prediction of outcomes in various scenarios. By assigning a numerical value to the likelihood of an event occurring, probability allows us to make educated guesses and assessments in the face of incomplete information. For instance, probability can be employed to determine the likelihood of a fair coin landing heads up, the possibility of rain tomorrow, or the risk of a computer system malfunctioning due to a specific error.

In the context of computer science, probability plays a crucial role in numerous areas, such as artificial intelligence, machine learning, and network reliability. Probability helps computer scientists design algorithms and systems that can adapt to and operate effectively in unpredictable environments by providing a rigorous framework for modelling and reasoning about uncertainty.

Statistics, conversely, is concerned with the gathering, analysis, interpretation, presentation, and organisation of data. It offers a robust set of tools and techniques for extracting meaningful insights and making inferences about larger populations based on samples of data. For example, statistics can be utilised to calculate the average age of people in a particular country, assess the effectiveness of a new software feature by analysing user feedback, or predict the outcome of an election based on polling data.

Moreover, statistics plays a vital role in various aspects of computer science, such as data analysis, data mining, and performance evaluation. By providing methods for quantifying relationships, trends, and patterns within data, statistics enable computer scientists to make data-driven decisions, build predictive models, and evaluate the effectiveness of their solutions.

To summarise, probability and statistics are two intertwined branches of mathematics that offer valuable tools for understanding and managing uncertainty and organising and interpreting data. They play a significant role in computer science, helping us make informed decisions, predictions, and generalisations in complex situations with incomplete information.

This chapter will explore the fascinating world of probability and statistics, covering essential concepts such as probability spaces, conditional probability, random variables, and probability distributions. We will also discuss deviation from the mean, and random walks, and delve into statistical inference and hypothesis testing. Lastly, we will learn about regression analysis, a powerful tool for understanding relationships between variables.

PROBABILITY

Probability is a fundamental mathematical concept that helps us measure the likelihood of certain events occurring in uncertain situations. It provides a quantitative framework for making predictions and informed decisions in the face of uncertain outcomes. In this section, we will introduce the essential principles and concepts of probability, starting with the basics of sample space, types of events, and properties of probability.

We will then explore the addition and multiplication rules of probability, which help us calculate the probabilities of the compound and mutually exclusive events. As we delve deeper, we will discuss conditional probability, dependent events, and Bayes' theorem, which are crucial for understanding the relationships between different events. Moreover, we will cover random variables, probability distributions, and various probability models, such as binomial and geometric probabilities.

Throughout this section, we will learn to apply probability theory to various real-world scenarios, from simple coin tosses and dice rolls to more complex situations like network reliability and decision-making under uncertainty. By the end of this section, you will have a solid understanding of the principles of probability and how they can be used to analyse and solve problems in various contexts.

SAMPLE SPACE AND TYPES OF EVENTS

The sample space, denoted as S or Ω, is the set of all possible outcomes of a random experiment. For example, when flipping a coin, the sample space is S = {Heads, Tails}. An event is a subset of the sample space. Events can be classified as simple (consisting of a single outcome, e.g., getting Heads), compound (consisting of multiple outcomes, e.g., getting Heads or Tails), mutually exclusive (events that cannot occur at the same time, e.g., getting both Heads and Tails), or complementary (events covering all possible outcomes, e.g., getting either Heads or Tails).

BASIC PROPERTIES OF PROBABILITY

Probability is a numerical measure of the likelihood of an event occurring, ranging from 0 (impossible) to 1 (certain). There are three basic properties of probability: (1) the probability of an event is always between 0 and 1, inclusive; (2) the probability of the entire sample space (i.e., the set of all possible outcomes) is 1; and (3) the sum of probabilities of all mutually exclusive events in a sample space is 1.

ADDITION RULE AND MUTUALLY EXCLUSIVE EVENTS

The addition rule states that the probability of either of two events occurring (A or B) is the sum of their individual probabilities minus the probability of both events occurring: $P(A \cup B) = P(A) + P(B) - P(A \cap B)$. Suppose the events are mutually exclusive (i.e., they cannot occur simultaneously). In that case, the probability of either event occurring is simply the sum of their individual probabilities: $P(A \cup B) = P(A) + P(B)$.

MULTIPLICATION RULE AND INDEPENDENT EVENTS

The multiplication rule states that the probability of two events occurring together (A and B) is the product of their individual probabilities and the probability of their intersection: $P(A \cap B) = P(A) \times P(B \mid A)$. Suppose the events are independent (i.e., the occurrence of one event does not affect the probability of the other). In that case, the probability of both events occurring is simply the product of their individual probabilities: $P(A \cap B) = P(A) \times P(B)$.

CONDITIONAL PROBABILITY AND DEPENDENT EVENTS

Conditional probability is the probability of an event occurring, given that another event has occurred. It is denoted as $P(A \mid B)$, meaning the probability of event A happening, given that event B has happened. Dependent events are events whose probabilities are influenced by the occurrence of other events. For example, the probability of drawing a red card from a deck of playing cards is dependent on whether a red card was drawn in the previous turn.

BAYES' THEOREM

Bayes' theorem is a fundamental rule in probability theory that allows us to update our beliefs based on new evidence. It states that the probability of an event A occurring, given that event B has occurred, is equal to the probability of event B occurring, given that event A has occurred, multiplied by the probability of event A, and divided by the probability of event B: $P(A|B) = (P(B|A) \times P(A)) / P(B)$.

COMPLEMENTARY EVENTS AND PROBABILITY

Complementary events are mutually exclusive and exhaustive events, meaning that if one occurs, the other cannot, and vice versa. The probability of a complementary event is equal to one minus the probability of the original event: $P(A') = 1 - P(A)$. Probability without replacement refers to situations where an item is not replaced after being selected, which can affect the probabilities of subsequent events. For example, drawing cards from a deck without replacing them changes the probability of drawing specific cards after each draw.

RANDOM VARIABLES AND DISTRIBUTIONS

A random variable is a function that assigns numerical values to the outcomes of a random experiment. A probability distribution is a function that describes the likelihood of different values for a random variable. Common probability distributions include the binomial distribution, which models the number of successes in a fixed number of Bernoulli trials (e.g., the number of heads in ten coin flips), and the geometric distribution, which models the number of trials needed for the first success in a sequence of Bernoulli trials (e.g., the number of coin flips needed to get the first head).

DEVIATION FROM THE MEAN

Deviation from the mean is a measure of how much a random variable's value varies from its expected value or average. It is an important concept in probability and statistics, as it helps us understand the dispersion and variability of data. For example, if we know the mean height of a group of people, the deviation from the mean would tell us how much individual heights differ from the average.

RANDOM WALKS

A random walk is a mathematical model that describes a path consisting of a succession of random steps. It is often used to model real-world phenomena, such as stock market fluctuations or the movement of particles in a fluid. For example, a simple one-dimensional random walk might involve a person taking steps forward or backwards along a straight line, with each step's direction determined by the flip of a coin.

THEORETICAL AND EXPERIMENTAL PROBABILITY

Theoretical probability is the likelihood of an event occurring based on mathematical principles and assumptions, whereas experimental probability is the likelihood of an event occurring based on observed outcomes from repeated experiments. For example, the theoretical probability of getting heads when flipping a fair coin is 1/2, while the experimental probability might be the actual proportion of heads observed in a series of coin flips.

AXIOMATIC PROBABILITY

Axiomatic probability is a formal approach to probability theory based on a set of axioms, which are basic assumptions or principles that underlie the theory. It provides a rigorous foundation for probability, allowing us to derive various rules and theorems, such as the addition and multiplication rules. The three primary axioms of probability are: (1) the probability of an event is always between 0 and 1, inclusive; (2) the probability of the entire sample space is 1; and (3) the sum of probabilities of all mutually exclusive events in a sample space is 1.

LAW OF LARGE NUMBERS

The Law of Large Numbers is an essential concept in probability that demonstrates the long-term stability of probabilities. It states that as the number of independent trials of a random experiment increases, the observed relative frequency of an event converges to its theoretical probability. For example, if you flip a fair coin many times, the proportion of heads (experimental probability) will approach 1/2 (theoretical probability) as the number of flips increases.

Incorporating this concept into the introductory knowledge of probability for non-CSE students helps them understand that while individual outcomes may be unpredictable, the overall behaviour of many trials becomes more predictable and stable. This idea is crucial in many real-world applications, such as insurance, finance, and statistical analysis.

STATISTICS

Statistics is a vital branch of mathematics that focuses on data collection, analysis, interpretation, presentation, and organisation. In computer science, statistics is crucial, including data analysis, machine learning, performance evaluation, and decision-making processes. For non-CSE students, it is essential to understand the foundational concepts of statistics to gain insights into the methods and techniques used by computer scientists to analyse and draw conclusions from data.

For instance, in developing a software application, statistical methods can help determine the average time it takes to load a page, the proportion of users who experience errors, or the relationship between the usage of specific features and user satisfaction. Similarly, in machine learning and artificial intelligence, statistical models are employed to make predictions and decisions based on historical data.

In this section, we will explore various topics in statistics that will provide non-CSE students with a strong foundation to understand its applications in computer science. The topics to be covered include descriptive statistics, data handling and presentation, probability distributions, sampling and sampling distributions, confidence intervals and hypothesis testing, regression analysis, and non-parametric statistics. By understanding these concepts, students will be better equipped to appreciate the role of statistics in computer science and its real-world applications.

DESCRIPTIVE STATISTICS

Descriptive statistics summarise a dataset's main features, helping us understand the data's general characteristics. These measures can be divided into three categories: measures of central tendency, measures of dispersion, and measures of association.

MEASURES OF CENTRAL TENDENCY

Central tendency measures give us a single value that represents the "centre" of a dataset.

Mean: The mean, often referred to as the average, is the sum of all data points divided by the total number of data points. For example, if we have test scores of 60, 70, 80, and 90, the mean would be (60+70+80+90)/4 = 75.

Median: The median is the middle value of a dataset when the data points are sorted in ascending order. If there's an odd number of data points, the median is the middle value; if even, the median is the average of the two middle values. In our test scores example, the median would be (70+80)/2 = 75.

Mode: The mode is the value that appears most frequently in a dataset. In our test scores example, if we have an additional score of 70, the mode would be 70, as it occurs twice.

MEASURES OF DISPERSION

Dispersion measures help us understand the spread or variability of data points in a dataset.

Range: The range is the difference between the highest and lowest values in a dataset. In our test scores example, the range would be 90 - 60 = 30.

Variance: Variance measures the average squared difference of each data point from the mean. In our example, the variance would be $((60-75)^2 + (70-75)^2 + (80-75)^2 + (90-75)^2)/4 = 125$.

Standard Deviation: The standard deviation is the square root of the variance. In our example, the standard deviation would be $\sqrt{125} \approx 11.18$.

MEASURES OF ASSOCIATION

Association measures help us understand the relationship between variables in a dataset.

Correlation: Correlation measures the strength and direction of a linear relationship between two variables. It ranges from -1 (perfect negative correlation) to 1 (perfect positive correlation), with 0 indicating no correlation.

Covariance: Covariance measures the degree to which two variables vary together. A positive covariance indicates that the variables tend to increase or decrease together, while a negative covariance suggests that one variable increases when the other decreases.

GRAPHICAL REPRESENTATION OF DATA

Graphical representation helps us visually summarise and understand the data.

Histograms: A histogram is a bar chart representing the distribution of a continuous variable, where the data is divided into intervals (bins), and the height of each bar corresponds to the frequency of data points within that interval.

Box and Whisker Plots: A box and whisker plot displays the distribution of a dataset using the median, quartiles, and extreme values. The "box" represents the interquartile range (IQR), while the "whiskers" extend to the minimum and maximum values within 1.5 times the IQR.

Scatter Plots: A scatter plot is a graphical representation of the relationship between two continuous variables. Each data point is plotted as a point in a two-dimensional space, with one variable on the x-axis and the other on the y-axis.

DATA HANDLING AND PRESENTATION

Effective data handling and presentation in computer science are crucial for making informed decisions based on the available data. Data handling and presentation involve organising, summarising, and visually representing data for better understanding and interpretation. Below are some key concepts related to data handling and presentation.

FREQUENCY DISTRIBUTION TABLE

A frequency distribution table is a method of organising and summarising raw data into a table format. It displays the frequencies of different values or ranges of values (called intervals) within a dataset. For example, a frequency distribution table of test scores might show the number of students who scored within specific grade ranges (e.g., 50-59, 60-69, 70-79, etc.).

RELATIVE FREQUENCY

Relative frequency is the ratio of the frequency of a specific value or interval to the total number of observations in a dataset. It helps to understand the proportion of occurrences of a specific value or interval in the dataset. For example, if there are 50 students and 10 of them scored between 70 and 79, the relative frequency for that range would be 10/50 or 0.2 (20%).

FIVE NUMBER SUMMARY

The five number summary is a set of five descriptive statistics that provide a quick overview of the distribution of a dataset. It consists of the minimum value, first quartile (Q_1), median (Q_2 or second quartile), third quartile (Q_3), and maximum value. The five number summary can be used to create a box and whisker plot, which visually represents the distribution and spread of the data.

UNGROUPED AND GROUPED DATA

Ungrouped data refers to raw data that has not been organised or summarised into groups or categories. It is the initial form of the data as collected. On the other hand, grouped data is the data that has been organised into groups or categories, usually by creating intervals. Grouping data helps to simplify and understand large datasets by reducing the number of individual data points and summarising the data in a more manageable form. For example, a dataset containing the ages of 100 people can be grouped into intervals of 10 years each (e.g., 0-9, 10-19, 20-29, etc.), making it easier to analyse and interpret.

PROBABILITY DISTRIBUTIONS

Probability distributions describe the likelihood of different outcomes or values occurring within a given dataset or random process. They can be used to make predictions and analyse uncertainty in various applications, including computer science. Below are some key concepts related to probability distributions.

DISCRETE PROBABILITY DISTRIBUTIONS

Discrete probability distributions describe the probabilities of distinct outcomes or values in a discrete random variable (i.e., a variable that can only take a finite or countable number of values). Some common discrete probability distributions include:

Binomial distribution: It describes the number of successes in a fixed number of independent Bernoulli trials, each having the same probability of success. For example, the number of heads obtained in 10 coin tosses follows a binomial distribution.

Poisson distribution: It represents the number of events occurring in a fixed interval of time or space, given a constant average rate of occurrence. For example, the number of emails received per hour in a mailbox follows a Poisson distribution.

Geometric distribution: It models the number of trials needed to obtain the first success in a sequence of independent Bernoulli trials. For example, the number of coin tosses before obtaining the first head follows a geometric distribution.

Continuous Probability Distributions

Continuous probability distributions describe the probabilities of outcomes or values in a continuous random variable (i.e., a variable that can take any value within a specified range or interval). Some common continuous probability distributions include:

Normal distribution: Also known as the Gaussian distribution, it is a symmetric bell-shaped distribution that describes many natural phenomena, including measurement errors, heights, and IQ scores. In computer science, it is often used to model noise and uncertainties.

Exponential distribution: It models the time between events in a Poisson process, where events occur continuously and independently at a constant average rate. For example, the time between consecutive logins to a website follows an exponential distribution.

Uniform distribution: It represents a random variable where all outcomes within a specified range are equally likely. For example, the time it takes for a computer to process a task within a given range can be modelled by a uniform distribution.

Empirical Rule and Degree of Freedom

Empirical Rule: Also known as the 68-95-99.7 rule, it states that in a normal distribution, approximately 68% of the data falls within one standard deviation of the mean, 95% falls within two standard deviations, and 99.7% falls within three standard deviations. This rule helps in understanding the dispersion of data in a normally distributed dataset.

Degree of Freedom: The degree of freedom refers to the number of independent pieces of information available for estimating a statistical parameter. It is an essential concept in hypothesis testing and the calculation of confidence intervals. For example, when calculating the sample variance of a dataset, the degrees of freedom are n-1, where n is the number of data points. This is because one degree of freedom is used up in estimating the mean, leaving n-1 independent pieces of information for estimating the variance.

SAMPLING AND SAMPLING DISTRIBUTIONS

Sampling and sampling distributions deal with the process of selecting a subset of individuals or items from a population to make inferences about the entire population. Sampling techniques are used to estimate population parameters, such as the mean, median, or proportion, based on the characteristics of the sample.

POPULATION AND SAMPLE

A population refers to the entire set of items or individuals of interest, while a sample is a subset of the population chosen for analysis. For example, if we want to study the average height of university students in the UK, the population would be all university students in the UK, and a sample would be a smaller group of students selected from various universities.

SIMPLE RANDOM SAMPLING

Simple random sampling is a technique in which each item or individual in the population has an equal chance of being included in the sample. For example, using a random number generator to select a group of students from a class.

STRATIFIED SAMPLING

Stratified sampling involves dividing the population into distinct groups or strata based on specific characteristics, such as age or gender. Then, a simple random sample is taken from each group. This method ensures that each group is well-represented in the sample, which can improve the accuracy of the estimations.

Systematic Sampling

In systematic sampling, a fixed interval selects items or individuals from the population. For example, every 10th student is selected from an ordered list of students. This method can be more efficient than simple random sampling but may introduce bias if the population has a systematic pattern.

Central Limit Theorem

The Central Limit Theorem is a fundamental statistical concept that states that, regardless of the underlying population distribution, the distribution of sample means will approach a normal distribution as the sample size increases. This theorem is important because it allows us to make inferences about the population based on sample data using standard statistical techniques.

Confidence Intervals and Hypothesis Testing

Confidence intervals and hypothesis testing are statistical methods used to make inferences about population parameters using sample data. Confidence intervals estimate the range within which a population parameter is likely to lie, while hypothesis testing evaluates the evidence supporting a claim about the population.

Confidence Interval for a Mean and Proportion

A confidence interval is a range of values within which a population parameter, such as the mean or proportion, is likely to fall. For example, a 95% confidence interval for the average height of university students might be (170 cm, 175 cm), indicating that we are 95% confident that the true average height lies within this range.

Comparing Two Means and Proportions

When comparing two populations, we may be interested in the difference between their means or proportions. Statistical tests, such as the t-test for means or the z-test for proportions, can be used to determine whether the differences are statistically significant or likely due to chance.

Null and Alternative Hypotheses

Hypothesis testing involves collecting evidence from sample data to determine whether to reject the null hypothesis in favour of the alternative hypothesis. The null hypothesis (H0) is a statement that there is no difference or effect between the populations being compared. The alternative hypothesis (H1) is the statement that there is a difference or effect.

TYPE I AND TYPE II ERRORS

A Type I error occurs when the null hypothesis is incorrectly rejected, while a Type II error occurs when the null hypothesis is incorrectly accepted. The significance level (α) is the probability of making a Type I error, and the power ($1 - \beta$) is the probability of correctly rejecting the null hypothesis when it is false.

SIGNIFICANCE LEVEL AND P-VALUE

The significance level (α) is the threshold below which we reject the null hypothesis in favour of the alternative hypothesis. A common choice is $\alpha = 0.05$, meaning there is a 5% chance of committing a Type I error. The p-value is the probability of observing the sample data or more extreme results, assuming the null hypothesis is true. If the p-value is less than or equal to α, we reject the null hypothesis.

ONE-SAMPLE AND TWO-SAMPLE TESTS

One-sample tests involve comparing a sample statistic to a known population parameter, while two-sample tests compare the statistics of two independent samples. Examples include the one-sample t-test for means, the two-sample t-test for comparing means, and the chi-square test for comparing proportions.

CATEGORICAL DATA AND CHI-SQUARE TEST

Categorical data is data that can be classified into distinct categories, such as gender or employment status. The chi-square test is used to determine whether there is a significant association between two categorical variables. For example, we could use the chi-square test to examine the relationship between gender and the choice of a programming language.

REGRESSION ANALYSIS

Regression analysis is a statistical technique used to model the relationship between a dependent variable and one or more independent variables. It helps us to predict future values of the dependent variable based on the values of the independent variables.

SIMPLE LINEAR REGRESSION

Simple linear regression is a type of regression analysis that models the relationship between a single independent variable (x) and a dependent variable (y) using a straight line, also known as the regression line. The regression line equation is $y = a + bx$, where a is the intercept and b is the slope.

MULTIPLE LINEAR REGRESSION

Multiple linear regression is an extension of simple linear regression that models the relationship between multiple independent variables (x_1, x_2, ..., x_n) and a dependent variable (y). The equation of the multiple regression line is $y = a + b_1x_1 + b_2x_2 + ... + b_nx_n$.

COEFFICIENT OF DETERMINATION (R-SQUARED)

The coefficient of determination, also known as R-squared, is a measure of how well the regression line fits the data. It ranges from 0 to 1, with higher values indicating a better fit. An R-squared value of 1 indicates that the regression line perfectly explains the variation in the dependent variable, while a value of 0 means that the line has no explanatory power.

NON-PARAMETRIC STATISTICS

Non-parametric statistics are statistical methods that make fewer assumptions about the underlying distribution of the data. They are useful when dealing with data that does not meet the assumptions of parametric tests, such as normality or homogeneity of variance.

Mann-Whitney U Test

The Mann-Whitney U test is a non-parametric test used to compare the central tendencies of two independent samples when the data is not normally distributed. It is the non-parametric equivalent of the independent samples t-test.

Kruskal-Wallis Test

The Kruskal-Wallis test is a non-parametric test used to compare the central tendencies of three or more independent samples when the data is not normally distributed. It is the non-parametric equivalent of the one-way analysis of variance (ANOVA).

Chapter 4 Exercises and More

Below you will find a set of practice questions and their corresponding answers. In addition, this section includes key takeaways and symbols from the chapter to help reinforce your understanding of the material.

Practice Questions

1. Define the terms "sample space" and "event" in the context of probability. Provide an example for each.
2. Explain the difference between descriptive and inferential statistics, and give an example of a situation where each would be used.
3. What are the three measures of central tendency, and how are they calculated? Provide an example of when you might use each measure.
4. What is the difference between a discrete and a continuous probability distribution? Provide an example for each.
5. In the context of hypothesis testing, explain the concepts of Type I and Type II errors. Which error occurs when the null hypothesis is rejected when it is actually true?
6. Explain the purpose of a confidence interval and how to interpret it. Provide an example of a confidence interval for the mean.
7. Describe the process of simple random sampling and explain its advantages and disadvantages.
8. What is the chi-square test, and when is it used? Provide an example of a situation where the chi-square test would be appropriate.
9. Explain the concept of regression analysis and the difference between simple linear regression and multiple linear regression. Provide an example of a situation where multiple linear regression would be more appropriate than simple linear regression.

10. What are non-parametric statistics, and when might you choose to use a non-parametric test like the Mann-Whitney U or Kruskal-Wallis test? Provide an example of a situation where a non-parametric test would be appropriate.

KEY TAKEAWAYS

- Probability is the study of the likelihood of various outcomes occurring in uncertain situations, and it helps make predictions and informed decisions.
- Statistics is the collection, analysis, interpretation, presentation, and organisation of data, which helps draw conclusions and make inferences about a population based on a sample of data.
- Descriptive statistics summarise and describe the main features of a dataset, including measures of central tendency (mean, median, mode), dispersion (range, variance, standard deviation), and graphical representation of data.
- Probability distributions can be classified into discrete (e.g., binomial, Poisson) and continuous (e.g., normal, exponential) distributions, depending on the nature of the random variable.
- The Central Limit Theorem states that the sampling distribution of the sample mean approaches a normal distribution as the sample size increases, regardless of the shape of the population distribution.
- Confidence intervals provide an estimated range of values within which a population parameter is likely to fall, with a specified confidence level (e.g., 95% confidence level).
- Hypothesis testing involves generalising about a population based on a sample and assessing the evidence against the null hypothesis in favour of the alternative hypothesis.
- Regression analysis models the relationship between variables, with simple linear regression involving one predictor variable and one outcome variable, and multiple linear regression involving multiple predictor variables.

- Non-parametric statistical tests, such as the Mann-Whitney U and Kruskal-Wallis tests, are used when the data do not meet the assumptions required for parametric tests, especially when dealing with non-normally distributed data.
- Probability and statistics are essential tools in computer science, as they provide the foundation for data analysis, machine learning, and decision-making under uncertainty.

ANSWERS TO THE PRACTICE QUESTIONS

1. A sample space is the set of all possible outcomes of a random experiment, while an event is a subset of the sample space, representing one or more outcomes. For example, in a coin toss, the sample space is {Heads, Tails}, and an event could be getting a "Heads."
2. Descriptive statistics summarize and describe the main features of a dataset, while inferential statistics use sample data to make generalizations about the population. Descriptive statistics might be used to describe the average age of a class, whereas inferential statistics might be used to estimate the average age of all students in a university.
3. The three measures of central tendency are mean (the arithmetic average), median (the middle value), and mode (the most frequently occurring value). You might use the mean to calculate the average salary of employees, the median to find the middle house price in a neighbourhood, and the mode to determine the most popular ice cream flavour.
4. A discrete probability distribution deals with discrete random variables (countable outcomes), such as the number of heads in coin tosses. A continuous probability distribution deals with continuous random variables (uncountable outcomes), such as the height of people. Examples: binomial distribution (discrete), normal distribution (continuous).

5. Type I error occurs when the null hypothesis is rejected when it is true (false positive). Type II error occurs when the null hypothesis is not rejected when it is false (false negative). Type I error is the error that occurs when the null hypothesis is rejected when it is true.
6. A confidence interval provides an estimated range of values within which the population parameter is likely to fall. For example, a 95% confidence interval for the mean age of a population might be 30-40 years, meaning we are 95% confident that the true mean age falls within this range.
7. Simple random sampling involves selecting a sample from a population such that each member has an equal chance of being included. Advantages: unbiased, easy to implement. Disadvantages: may not be representative if the sample size is small or the population is diverse.
8. The chi-square test is used to determine if there is a significant association between two categorical variables. For example, you could use the chi-square test to see if there is a relationship between the type of degree and the likelihood of securing a job.
9. Regression analysis is used to investigate the relationship between variables. Simple linear regression involves one predictor variable and one outcome variable, while multiple linear regression involves multiple predictor variables. Multiple linear regression would be more appropriate when trying to predict a house price based on multiple factors, such as square footage and location.
10. Non-parametric statistics do not assume a specific distribution for the data and are used when the data do not meet the assumptions required for parametric tests. You might choose to use the Mann-Whitney U test when comparing two independent samples with non-normally distributed data or the Kruskal-Wallis test when comparing more than two independent samples with non-normally distributed data.

SYMBOLS TO REMEMBER

Here is a list of some common symbols used in Chapter 4, covering Probability and Statistics:

- P(A) - Probability of event A
- P(A ∩ B) - Probability of event A and event B occurring together
- P(A ∪ B) - Probability of event A or event B occurring
- P(A | B) - Conditional probability of event A given event B
- P(A' | B) - Conditional probability of the complement of event A given event B
- P(A ∩ B') - Probability of event A and the complement of event B occurring together
- μ - Population mean
- $\bar{x}$ - Sample mean
- σ - Population standard deviation
- s - Sample standard deviation
- σ^2 - Population variance
- s^2 - Sample variance
- n - Sample size
- N - Population size
- ρ - Population correlation coefficient
- r - Sample correlation coefficient
- X^2 - Chi-square statistic
- α - Significance level
- p - P-value
- θ - Population proportion
- π - Sample proportion
- f(x) - Probability density function
- F(x) - Cumulative distribution function
- E(X) - Expected value of a random variable X
- Var(X) - Variance of a random variable X
- SD(X) - Standard deviation of a random variable X

CHAPTER 5

OPTIMISATION AND APPLICATIONS OF MATHEMATICS

This chapter delves into optimisation, a vital branch of mathematics that focuses on finding the best possible solution to a problem, often subject to certain constraints. Optimisation techniques are widely used in various fields, including computer science, engineering, operations research, and economics. In this chapter, we will explore different optimisation methods, their applications, and their relevance to the world of computing.

Optimisation plays a crucial role in solving complex problems and enhancing the performance of systems and processes. In the context of computing, optimisation techniques are employed to improve the efficiency of algorithms, balance resource allocation, and design cost-effective networks, among other applications. As computational resources are finite, it is essential to make the most efficient use of them in order to solve problems effectively and quickly. This chapter will provide insight into how optimisation techniques can be utilised to achieve these goals, helping to bridge the gap between theory and practice.

Furthermore, this chapter aims to demonstrate the versatility and utility of mathematical concepts in addressing real-world challenges. By examining various case studies and examples, readers will not only grasp the fundamental principles of optimisation but also develop an appreciation for the power and relevance of mathematics in computing. As you progress through this chapter, you will discover how mathematical concepts can be adapted and applied to various problems, equipping you with the knowledge and skills to tackle similar challenges in your own work or studies.

OPTIMISATION

The optimisation involves finding the best possible solution to a problem, given a specific objective function and certain constraints. In mathematical terms, optimisation deals with maximising or minimising the value of an objective function while adhering to the defined constraints. This process is crucial in various fields, such as computer science, engineering, operations research, and economics.

There are two main types of optimisation problems: local and global.

LOCAL OPTIMUM

A local optimum is an optimal solution within a limited search space. Local optimum is an optimal solution within a restricted or limited search space. In other words, it is a point at which the objective function's value is either a minimum or maximum compared to other nearby points, but not necessarily the overall minimum or maximum. Identifying local optima is crucial in many optimisation problems, as they can provide insights into potential solutions and areas of interest.

Example 1: Imagine you are trying to find the highest point on hilly terrain. You start walking and reach the top of a small hill. From your perspective, this is a local optimum, as it is the highest point in your immediate vicinity. However, taller hills could be nearby, which you can only discover by exploring further. In this case, the local optimum does not necessarily represent the highest point in the entire terrain.

Example 2: Consider a company that wants to minimise the production cost of a product. They have several production facilities, each with its own cost structure. By analysing the cost function for each facility, they find that Facility A has the lowest cost among all facilities, but only for a specific range of production volumes. This represents a local optimum for the production cost. However, when the company considers the entire range of production volumes, they might find that Facility B offers a lower overall cost, which would be the global optimum. In this scenario, the local optimum provides valuable information, but it is not the ultimate solution to the problem.

GLOBAL OPTIMUM

A global optimum is the best solution across the entire search space. Finding global optima can be challenging due to the complexity of the problem or the presence of numerous local optima that may mislead the optimisation process.

Example 1: A bakery wants to determine the ideal quantity of ingredients to maximise profit while considering the cost of raw materials and the prices of finished goods. The objective function is the total profit, and the constraints include the available budget and the cost of ingredients.

Example 2: A delivery company aims to minimise the total distance travelled by its fleet of vehicles to deliver packages to various destinations. The objective function is the total distance, and the constraints include the number of available vehicles and the maximum distance each vehicle can travel.

LINEAR PROGRAMMING AND ITS APPLICATIONS

Linear programming is an optimisation technique for problems with a linear objective function and linear constraints. Given the constraints, the goal is to find the optimal value of the objective function. Linear programming problems can be solved using various methods, such as simplex and graphical solutions.

Graphical solutions involve visually representing the constraints on a two-dimensional plane and identifying the feasible region that satisfies all constraints. The optimal solution lies at the vertices of this region. The simplex method is an iterative algorithm that starts with an initial feasible solution and gradually moves towards the optimal solution by improving the objective function value at each step.

Example 1: A manufacturer produces two products, A and B, using the same set of resources. The company aims to maximise its profit while considering both products' production costs and selling prices. The objective function is the total profit, and the constraints include the availability of resources and production capacities.

Example 2: A farmer must allocate a limited budget to buy seeds for planting two crops, X and Y. The goal is to maximise the total yield, considering the cost of seeds, the expected yield per seed, and the available budget. The objective function is the total yield, and the constraints include the budget limit and the cost of seeds.

As mentioned earlier, linear programming is an optimisation technique that deals with problems with a linear objective function and linear constraints. In addition to graphical solutions and the simplex method, other methods and variations of linear programming can be useful in different scenarios.

Dual Linear Programming

Dual linear programming is a counterpart to the original (primal) linear programming problem. It involves transforming the primal problem into another linear programming problem, called the dual problem. Solving the dual problem can provide insights into the primal problem, such as bounds on the optimal solution and sensitivity analysis.

Example: A transportation company needs to minimise the total cost of shipping goods from multiple factories to multiple warehouses. The dual problem could provide insights into the impact of changes in shipping costs on the optimal solution.

Integer Linear Programming

Integer linear programming is a variant of linear programming in which the decision variables are restricted to integer values. This type of problem is generally more difficult to solve than regular linear programming problems due to the additional integer constraints.

Example: A company must determine the optimal number of employees to assign to various tasks, ensuring that the total workload is completed within a given time frame. The decision variables (number of employees) must be integers.

Mixed-Integer Linear Programming

Mixed-integer linear programming is a combination of linear programming and integer linear programming, in which some decision variables are required to be integers while others can take continuous values.

Example: A manufacturing plant needs to decide on the optimal production quantities of multiple products, some of which require integer quantities (e.g., whole units) and others that can be produced in continuous amounts (e.g., litres or kilograms).

MULTI-OBJECTIVE LINEAR PROGRAMMING

Multi-objective linear programming deals with problems that have more than one objective function. In these cases, the goal is to find solutions representing trade-offs between the various objectives.

Example: A city planner must allocate resources to different public services, such as healthcare, education, and transportation, aiming to maximise the overall quality of life for residents. The planner must consider multiple objectives: service quality, accessibility, and cost-effectiveness.

NONLINEAR OPTIMISATION

Nonlinear optimisation deals with problems where the objective function and/or the constraints are nonlinear. Nonlinear optimisation problems can be more challenging to solve than linear programming problems due to multiple local optima and the complexity of the objective function. Iterative methods, such as gradient descent and Newton's method, are commonly used to solve nonlinear optimisation problems.

Gradient descent is an algorithm that iteratively adjusts the solution toward the steepest decrease of the objective function. This process continues until the solution converges to a local minimum. Newton's method is an iterative algorithm that uses second-order information (the Hessian matrix) to determine the direction of improvement for the objective function.

Example 1: A company wants to determine the optimal price for a product to maximise revenue, considering the demand curve and the relationship between price and demand. The objective function is the total revenue, and the constraints might include the minimum and maximum prices the company can charge.

Example 2: In machine learning, a model's parameters need to be optimised to minimise the error between predicted and actual outcomes. The objective function is the error function, and the constraints include the model structure and the data available for training. In a neural network, for instance, the error function could be the mean squared error, and the optimisation process involves adjusting the weights and biases of the network to minimise the error.

As discussed, nonlinear optimisation involves problems with nonlinear objective functions and/or constraints. In addition to gradient descent and Newton's method, several other methods and concepts in nonlinear optimisation can be applied to various situations.

Constrained Nonlinear Optimisation: Constrained nonlinear optimisation deals with problems that have both nonlinear objective functions and constraints. Solving these problems often requires using specific algorithms, such as Sequential Quadratic Programming (SQP) and Barrier or Interior-Point methods.

Example: A chemical company needs to optimise the production process for a particular product to maximise the yield while adhering to safety regulations and environmental constraints. The objective function could be the yield, and the constraints could include temperature, pressure, and pollutant levels.

Unconstrained Nonlinear Optimisation

Unconstrained nonlinear optimisation problems involve a nonlinear objective function without any constraints. These problems can be solved using various algorithms, such as the steepest descent, conjugate gradient, and quasi-Newton methods.

Example: A software company wants to improve the performance of an algorithm by adjusting its parameters. The objective function might be the execution time of the algorithm, and the goal is to find the parameters that minimise the execution time.

Multi-objective Nonlinear Optimisation

Multi-objective nonlinear optimisation deals with problems with multiple nonlinear objective functions. These problems often require specific techniques, such as Pareto optimisation, to find solutions representing trade-offs between different objectives.

Example: A city planner must design a transportation network that maximises accessibility and minimises environmental impact. The planner must consider multiple nonlinear objectives, such as travel time, energy consumption, and emissions, to find a set of optimal solutions.

GLOBAL OPTIMISATION

Global optimisation algorithms aim to find the global optimum in nonlinear optimisation problems that have multiple local optima. These methods include techniques such as simulated annealing, genetic algorithms, and particle swarm optimisation.

Example: An engineering company needs to design an optimal structure for a bridge, considering factors like load capacity, material costs, and aesthetics. The objective function might be a combination of these factors, and the problem could involve multiple local optima, requiring a global optimisation technique to find the best overall solution.

OPTIMISATION ALGORITHMS

Optimisation algorithms are used to find the best solution to a problem when traditional methods are inadequate or when the problem involves a large search space. Some common optimisation algorithms include evolutionary algorithms, swarm intelligence, and simulated annealing.

Evolutionary algorithms, such as genetic algorithms, mimic the process of natural selection to find the optimal solution. They involve creating a population of candidate solutions and iteratively applying genetic operators, like mutation and crossover, to generate new solutions that perform better on the objective function.

Swarm intelligence algorithms, such as particle swarm optimisation, are inspired by the collective behaviour of social animals, like birds or insects. These algorithms model the movement of a swarm of particles or agents, each representing a potential solution, through the search space to find the best solution.

Simulated annealing is a stochastic optimisation algorithm inspired by the annealing process in metallurgy. The algorithm explores the search space by accepting new solutions with a probability that decreases as the search progresses, allowing it to escape local optima and converge to a global optimum.

Example 1: Genetic algorithms can be used to optimise complex engineering designs, such as designing an aerodynamic vehicle or an efficient wind turbine, by simulating the process of natural selection.

Example 2: Particle swarm optimisation can be employed to optimise the placement of wireless sensors in a network, considering factors like signal strength, coverage, and power consumption.

In addition to the mentioned optimisation algorithms, there are several other methods that can be applied to various situations, further expanding the range of possibilities in problem-solving.

TABU SEARCH

Tabu search is a metaheuristic algorithm that uses memory structures to guide the search for the optimal solution. By remembering previously visited solutions and imposing restrictions on the search space, tabu search can avoid cycling and escape local optima.

Example: Tabu search can be used for solving vehicle routing problems, where a fleet of vehicles must deliver goods to various locations while minimising the total distance travelled and adhering to capacity constraints.

ANT COLONY OPTIMISATION (ACO)

ACO is a swarm intelligence algorithm inspired by the foraging behaviour of ants. The algorithm simulates the pheromone trail left by ants, which guides other ants towards optimal paths. ACO has been widely used for solving combinatorial optimisation problems, such as the travelling salesman problem and the quadratic assignment problem.

Example: ACO can be applied to optimise the scheduling of tasks in a distributed computing environment, considering factors like task dependencies, resource allocation, and execution time.

HILL CLIMBING

Hill climbing is a local search algorithm that starts with an initial solution and iteratively moves towards the best neighbouring solution until it reaches a local optimum. Variants of hill climbing, such as stochastic hill climbing and random-restart hill climbing, have been developed to overcome the limitations of the basic algorithm.

Example: Hill climbing can be used for feature selection in machine learning, where the goal is to find a subset of input features that maximise the performance of a predictive model while reducing the dimensionality of the data.

DIFFERENTIAL EVOLUTION (DE)

DE is a population-based evolutionary algorithm that generates new candidate solutions by combining the differences between randomly selected individuals from the population. DE has been successfully applied to a wide range of continuous optimisation problems, such as function minimisation and parameter tuning.

Example: DE can be employed to optimise the design of an electrical circuit, considering factors like component values, power consumption, and signal integrity.

Mathematical Modelling in Computing

Mathematical modelling involves creating abstract representations of real-world problems using mathematical concepts and structures. In computing, mathematical models are crucial for understanding and solving complex problems. Creating a mathematical model involves identifying the relevant variables, defining their relationships, and formulating equations or algorithms to describe the system's behaviour.

Once a mathematical model is developed, it can be analysed and refined to improve its accuracy and effectiveness in solving the problem. Mathematical models are invaluable tools in computing for simulating, analysing, and optimising various systems and processes.

Example 1: In computer networks, mathematical models can simulate traffic patterns, congestion, and the effects of different network configurations on performance. This can help network administrators make informed decisions on resource allocation and network design.

Example 2: In software development, mathematical models can be used to estimate the cost, effort, and schedule of a project based on various factors, such as the size of the project, the complexity of the requirements, and the experience of the development team. This can help project managers plan and manage resources more effectively.

Machine Learning and Statistical Modelling

Machine learning is a subfield of artificial intelligence that focuses on developing algorithms that allow computers to learn from and make predictions or decisions based on data. Statistical modelling is the process of creating mathematical representations to describe, explain, or predict observed data. Both machine learning and statistical modelling play crucial roles in computing, as they enable the extraction of meaningful information from large datasets and facilitate decision-making.

In computing, machine learning and statistical modelling are used to develop models that can be trained on historical data and applied to new, unseen data for prediction, classification, or clustering tasks. By incorporating these techniques, computing systems can become more adaptive, intelligent, and efficient.

Example 1: In recommendation systems, machine learning algorithms can be used to predict a user's preferences based on their past behaviour and the behaviour of other users with similar interests. This allows the system to recommend products, services, or content that are more likely to be relevant and appealing to the user.

Example 2: In computer vision, statistical modelling techniques can be employed to identify patterns and features in images, such as edges, textures, or colours. By training machine learning models on labelled datasets, these algorithms can learn to recognise and classify objects, detect anomalies, or perform other vision tasks with high accuracy.

OPTIMISATION IN MACHINE LEARNING

Optimisation plays a significant role in machine learning, as many algorithms involve finding the best set of parameters to minimise an error or loss function. This process allows the model to generalise well and make accurate predictions on unseen data. Various optimisation techniques, such as gradient descent, Newton's method, or evolutionary algorithms, can be used to train machine learning models.

In computing, optimisation techniques are crucial for developing efficient and effective machine learning models that can be applied to various tasks, such as image recognition, natural language processing, or data analysis.

Example 1: In deep learning, neural networks are trained using gradient-based optimisation techniques, such as stochastic gradient descent or adaptive methods like Adam, to adjust the weights and biases of the network to minimise the error between the predicted and actual outcomes.

Example 2: In support vector machines, a type of supervised learning model, optimisation techniques are used to find the optimal hyperplane that maximises the margin between different classes. This enables the model to classify new data points with high accuracy and robustness.

APPLICATIONS OF MATHEMATICAL CONCEPTS AND TECHNIQUES IN VARIOUS FIELDS

Mathematics is a powerful tool that can be applied in many fields to solve problems, improve efficiency, and make informed decisions. In computer science and engineering, mathematical concepts and techniques are used to address various challenges, such as optimising algorithms, analysing data, and designing secure communication protocols.

Some common applications of mathematical concepts and techniques in computing include:

CRYPTOGRAPHY

Using number theory and algebra to develop secure encryption and decryption algorithms, ensuring secure data transmission and storage.

Cryptography protects information by transforming it into an unreadable format, ensuring secure transmission and storage. Cryptography utilises various mathematical concepts, including number theory and algebra, to develop secure encryption and decryption algorithms. Encryption involves transforming plaintext (readable data) into ciphertext (unreadable data) using a secret key, while decryption involves reversing this process using the same key to obtain the original plaintext. Cryptography is widely used in various fields, such as finance, healthcare, and government, to safeguard sensitive data.

Example 1: The Advanced Encryption Standard (AES) is a widely used encryption algorithm that employs mathematical operations, such as substitution and permutation, to transform plaintext into ciphertext. AES is used in secure communication protocols, such as Transport Layer Security (TLS) and Secure Sockets Layer (SSL), to protect data transmitted over networks.

Example 2: Cryptography is also used in digital signatures to ensure the authenticity and integrity of data. A digital signature involves transforming a message into a hash code using a hashing algorithm and encrypting the hash code using the sender's private key. The receiver can then verify the message's authenticity by decrypting the hash code using the sender's public key and comparing it to the original hash code.

IMAGE PROCESSING

Applying techniques from linear algebra, calculus, and statistics to process and manipulate digital images, enabling tasks such as image compression, filtering, and edge detection.

Image processing involves manipulating and analysing digital images using mathematical techniques. It utilises concepts from linear algebra, calculus, and statistics to process and enhance images, enabling tasks such as image compression, filtering, and edge detection. Image processing is widely used in various fields, such as medicine, remote sensing, and computer vision.

Example 1: The Sobel operator is a common edge detection filter used in image processing. It works by computing the gradient of the image using convolution with a small matrix (kernel), highlighting edges in the image.

Example 2: Image compression algorithms, such as JPEG and PNG, use mathematical techniques such as discrete cosine transform (DCT) and wavelet transform to reduce the size of image files without significant loss of image quality.

MACHINE LEARNING

Employing probability, statistics, and linear algebra concepts to develop algorithms that can learn from data, making predictions and decisions based on the acquired knowledge.

Machine learning involves developing algorithms that can learn from data and make predictions or decisions based on the acquired knowledge. It utilises various mathematical concepts, including probability, statistics, and linear algebra, to develop and refine these algorithms. Machine learning is widely used in various fields, such as finance, healthcare, and autonomous systems.

Example 1: In computer graphics, mathematical techniques are used to model and render three-dimensional objects, create realistic lighting and shading, and simulate physical phenomena such as fluid dynamics and particle systems.

Example 2: In bioinformatics, mathematical models and algorithms are employed to analyse and interpret biological data, such as DNA sequences and protein structures, leading to new insights in fields like genomics, proteomics, and drug discovery.

Chapter 5 Exercises and More

Below you will find a set of practice questions and their corresponding answers. In addition, this section includes key takeaways and symbols from the chapter to help reinforce your understanding of the material.

Practice Questions

1. What is the difference between local and global optima?
2. What is linear programming and how is it used in optimisation?
3. What is dual linear programming?
4. How does integer linear programming differ from mixed-integer linear programming?
5. What is nonlinear optimisation and what are some of the challenges in solving nonlinear optimisation problems?
6. What is the difference between unconstrained and multi-objective nonlinear optimisation?
7. What is the goal of global optimisation and what are some of the algorithms used to solve global optimisation problems?
8. What is mathematical modelling and how is it used in computing?
9. What are some applications of mathematical concepts in cryptography?
10. How is machine learning used in optimisation and what are some of the techniques used in machine learning and statistical modelling?

Key Takeaways

- The optimisation involves finding the best possible solution to a problem, given a specific objective function and certain constraints.

- There are two main types of optimisation problems: local and global. A local optimum is a solution that is optimal within a limited search space, while a global optimum is the best solution across the entire search space.
- Linear programming is an optimisation technique for problems with a linear objective function and linear constraints and can be solved using various methods such as simplex and graphical solutions.
- Nonlinear optimisation deals with problems where the objective function and/or the constraints are nonlinear, and iterative methods such as gradient descent and Newton's method are commonly used to solve them.
- Optimisation algorithms such as evolutionary algorithms, swarm intelligence, and simulated annealing can be used to find the best solution to a problem when traditional methods are inadequate or when the problem involves a large search space.
- Mathematical modelling involves creating abstract representations of real-world problems using mathematical concepts and structures and is a crucial tool in computing for simulating, analysing and optimising various systems and processes.
- Cryptography uses number theory and algebra to develop secure encryption and decryption algorithms, ensuring secure data transmission and storage.
- Image processing applies techniques from linear algebra, calculus, and statistics to process and manipulate digital images, enabling image compression, filtering, and edge detection tasks.
- Machine learning employs probability, statistics, and linear algebra concepts to develop algorithms that can learn from data, making predictions and decisions based on the acquired knowledge.
- Mathematical concepts and techniques are widely used in various fields, such as computer science, engineering, operations research, and economics, to solve complex problems and develop innovative solutions.

Symbols to Remember

- Sigma (Σ)
- Pi (Π)
- Less than or equal to (≤)
- Greater than or equal to (≥)
- Summation notation (Σ)
- Product notation (Π)
- Exponential notation (e)
- Derivative notation (dy/dx)
- Hessian matrix (H)
- Gradient notation (∇)
- Intersection (∩)
- Union (∪)
- Complement (A')
- Subset (⊆)
- Superset (⊇)
- Equals (=)
- Not equals (≠)
- Infinity (∞)
- Integer (ℤ)
- Natural numbers (ℕ)

Answer to the Practice Question

1. Local optima are optimal solutions within a limited search space, whereas global optima are the best possible solutions across the entire search space.
2. Linear programming is an optimisation technique for problems with a linear objective function and linear constraints. Given the constraints, it is used to find the optimal value of the objective function.
3. Dual linear programming is a method used to convert a maximisation problem into a minimisation problem, or vice versa.

4. Integer linear programming involves finding the optimal solution to a problem where the variables are restricted to be integers. In contrast, mixed-integer linear programming allows some variables to be continuous and others to be integers.
5. Nonlinear optimisation deals with problems with nonlinear objective functions and/or constraints. Challenges in solving these problems include multiple local optima and the complexity of the objective function.
6. Unconstrained nonlinear optimisation involves finding the optimal solution without any constraints, whereas multi-objective nonlinear optimisation simultaneously optimises multiple conflicting objectives.
7. Global optimisation aims to find the optimal or best solution across the entire search space. Some algorithms for global optimisation problems include tabu search, ant colony optimisation, hill climbing, and differential evolution.
8. Mathematical modelling involves creating abstract representations of real-world problems using mathematical concepts and structures. It is used in computing for simulating, analyzing, and optimising various systems and processes.
9. Mathematical concepts are used in cryptography to develop secure encryption and decryption algorithms, ensuring secure data transmission and storage.
10. Machine learning is used in optimisation to develop algorithms that can learn from data, making predictions and decisions based on the acquired knowledge. Machine learning and statistical modelling techniques include probability, statistics, and linear algebra concepts.

CHAPTER 6

Introduction to Boolean Algebra and Its Use in Digital Logic Circuits

Boolean algebra, a branch of mathematics developed by George Boole in the mid-19th century, deals with manipulating and analysing binary values (0 and 1), representing true and false or on and off states. This algebra forms the foundation of digital logic circuits, essential building blocks of digital systems such as computers and other electronic devices. As this book is aimed at non-CSE students, we will present the concepts in a way that is easy to understand, even for those without a technical background.

This chapter will explore the basics of Boolean algebra, including its operators and their respective truth tables. These operators, such as AND, OR, and NOT, allow us to perform logical operations on binary values. Furthermore, we will discuss De Morgan's laws, which help simplify complex Boolean expressions.

Next, we will delve into digital logic circuits, focusing on how they are designed using Boolean algebra. We will examine the various logic gates, such as AND, OR, and NOT gates, and their symbols. These gates form the foundation of more complex circuits, including combinational and sequential logic circuits.

Lastly, we will touch on the applications of Boolean algebra in various fields, such as cryptography and machine learning. By understanding the principles of Boolean algebra and digital logic circuits, you will gain a deeper appreciation for the inner workings of modern electronic devices and computer systems.

All in all, this chapter will provide a gentle introduction to Boolean algebra and its role in digital logic circuits. By the end of the chapter, you will have a solid understanding of the basic concepts and their applications, paving the way for further exploration of computer science engineering.

BOOLEAN OPERATORS AND THEIR TRUTH TABLES

Boolean operators are the fundamental building blocks of Boolean algebra, used to perform logical operations on binary values (0 and 1). There are three primary Boolean operators: AND, OR, and NOT. We'll explore these operators and their corresponding truth tables, which show the output of each operation based on all possible input combinations.

AND Operator

The AND operator, denoted by the symbol ∧, returns 1 (true) if both input values are 1, and 0 (false) otherwise.

Truth Table for AND

Input A	Input B	Output (A ∧ B)
0	0	0
0	1	0
1	0	0
1	1	1

OR Operator

The OR operator, denoted by the symbol ∨, returns 1 (true) if either or both input values are 1, and 0 (false) if both inputs are 0.

Truth Table for OR

Input A	Input B	Output (A ∨ B)
0	0	0
0	1	1
1	0	1
1	1	1

NOT OPERATOR

The NOT operator, denoted by the symbol ¬, is a unary operator, meaning it works on a single input value. It returns the negation of the input value, i.e., it inverts the binary value. If the input is 1 (true), the output is 0 (false), and vice versa.

TRUTH TABLE FOR NOT

Input A	Output (¬A)
0	1
1	0

These truth tables represent the basic behaviour of Boolean operators, which are the foundation for designing digital logic circuits and understanding more complex Boolean expressions.

DE MORGAN'S LAWS

De Morgan's laws are fundamental rules in Boolean algebra that describe the relationships between the AND, OR, and NOT operators. They are particularly useful for simplifying Boolean expressions and designing digital logic circuits. De Morgan's laws consist of two rules:

DE MORGAN'S FIRST LAW

The negation of the conjunction (AND) of two Boolean variables is equivalent to the disjunction (OR) of the negations of those variables. Mathematically, this can be represented as:

$\neg(A \land B) = (\neg A) \lor (\neg B)$

This means that if you have a Boolean expression with an AND operator and you want to negate the whole expression, you can instead negate the individual variables and use an OR operator between them.

DE MORGAN'S SECOND LAW

The negation of the disjunction (OR) of two Boolean variables is equivalent to the conjunction (AND) of the negations of those variables. Mathematically, this can be represented as:

$\neg(A \lor B) = (\neg A) \land (\neg B)$

This means that if you have a Boolean expression with an OR operator and you want to negate the whole expression, you can instead negate the individual variables and use an AND operator between them.

These laws are incredibly helpful in simplifying and transforming Boolean expressions, making it easier to understand and implement digital logic circuits. De Morgan's laws can also be extended to more than two variables, simplifying more complex Boolean expressions.

LOGIC GATES AND THEIR SYMBOLS

Logic gates are the fundamental building blocks of digital circuits. They perform basic logical operations using Boolean algebra, and their input and output values are either true (1) or false (0). Logic gates are essential components in digital systems, as they enable the processing and manipulation of binary data. This section will discuss the most common logic gates and their symbols.

AND Gate

The AND gate takes two or more input values and returns true (1) only if all input values are true. Its symbol is a flat, D-shaped figure with two or more inputs on the left and one output on the right.

OR Gate

The OR gate takes two or more input values and returns true (1) if at least one of the input values is true. Its symbol is a curved, D-shaped figure with two or more inputs on the left and one output on the right.

NOT Gate (Inverter)

The NOT gate, also known as an inverter, takes one input value and returns the opposite value. Its symbol is a triangle with a small circle on the right side, representing the inversion of the input value. If the input is true (1), the output is false (0), and vice versa.

NAND Gate

The NAND gate combines an AND gate followed by a NOT gate. Its symbol is similar to the AND gate but with a small circle on the right side, indicating the inversion of the AND operation. It takes two or more input values and returns false (0) only if all input values are true.

NOR Gate

The NOR gate is a combination of an OR gate followed by a NOT gate. Its symbol is similar to the OR gate but with a small circle on the right side, indicating the inversion of the OR operation. It takes two or more input values and returns true (1) only if all input values are false.

XOR Gate (Exclusive OR)

The XOR gate takes two input values and returns true (1) if exactly one of the input values is true. Its symbol is similar to the OR gate but has an additional curved line on the left.

XNOR Gate (Exclusive NOR)

The XNOR gate is a combination of an XOR gate followed by a NOT gate. Its symbol is similar to the XOR gate but with a small circle on the right side, indicating the inversion of the XOR operation. It takes two input values and returns true (1) if both input values are the same.

These logic gates are the basic building blocks of digital systems, and understanding their symbols and functions is crucial for anyone learning about digital logic circuits. Combining these gates in various configurations allows you to create more complex circuits capable of performing a wide range of tasks.

BOOLEAN EXPRESSIONS AND THEIR SIMPLIFICATION

Boolean expressions are mathematical representations of logical operations involving Boolean variables. These expressions can be simplified using a set of rules and laws derived from Boolean algebra. Simplifying Boolean expressions is essential for designing efficient digital circuits and reducing the complexity of the system. This section will discuss Boolean expressions and their simplification in an easy-to-understand manner for non-technical individuals.

BASIC BOOLEAN OPERATIONS

There are three fundamental operations in Boolean algebra: AND (represented as · or sometimes just by juxtaposition), OR (represented as +), and NOT (represented as ¬ or an overbar). These operations can be combined to create Boolean expressions. For example, given two Boolean variables A and B, we can have expressions like A·B, A+B, or ¬A.

LAWS OF BOOLEAN ALGEBRA

Boolean algebra is governed by a set of laws that can be used to manipulate and simplify Boolean expressions. Some essential laws include the Identity, Null, Idempotent, Commutative, Associative, Distributive, and De Morgan's laws. These laws allow us to transform Boolean expressions into simpler or equivalent forms.

SIMPLIFICATION TECHNIQUES

There are several techniques for simplifying Boolean expressions. Some common methods are:

a) Algebraic Simplification: Applying the laws of Boolean algebra to manipulate and reduce the expression to a simpler form.

b) Karnaugh Maps: A graphical representation of Boolean expressions that helps visualize patterns and simplify the expression by grouping terms.

c) Quine-McCluskey Algorithm: A tabular method for minimising Boolean expressions by identifying prime implicants and essential prime implicants.

Example of Boolean Expression Simplification:
Let's consider a Boolean expression $F = A \cdot B + \neg A \cdot B + \neg(A+B)$. To simplify this expression, we can follow these steps:

a) Apply De Morgan's law to the last term: $\neg(A+B) = \neg A \cdot \neg B$.

b) Rewrite the expression: $F = A \cdot B + \neg A \cdot B + \neg A \cdot \neg B$.

c) Factor out common terms: $F = B(A + \neg A) + \neg A \cdot \neg B$.

d) Apply the Identity law $(A + \neg A = 1)$: $F = B \cdot 1 + \neg A \cdot \neg B$.

e) Remove the redundant multiplication by 1: $F = B + \neg A \cdot \neg B$.

Now, the simplified Boolean expression is $F = B + \neg A \cdot \neg B$. Simplifying Boolean expressions can result in more efficient and less complex digital circuits, making it an essential skill for anyone working with digital logic.

Logic Gates and Their Use in Creating Complex Circuits

Logic gates are fundamental building blocks of digital circuits. They perform basic Boolean operations on input signals and produce an output based on the operation's rules. We can create complex circuits that perform more advanced functions by combining various logic gates. This section will explore logic gates and their use in creating complex circuits in an easy-to-understand manner for non-technical individuals.

Basic Logic Gates

Three primary logic gates correspond to the basic Boolean operations:

a) **AND Gate**: This gate has two or more inputs and produces an output of 1 (true) only when all its inputs are 1. Otherwise, the output is 0 (false).

b) **OR Gate:** This gate also has two or more inputs, and its output is 1 if at least one of its inputs is 1. The output is 0 only when all its inputs are 0.

c) **NOT Gate (Inverter):** This gate has only one input and inverts the input signal. If the input is 1, the output is 0, and vice versa.

Derived Logic Gates

Apart from the basic gates, there are other logic gates derived from combinations of the basic gates, such as:

a) **NAND Gate (NOT-AND):** This gate is an AND gate followed by a NOT gate. Its output is 1 when any of its inputs is 0.

b) NOR Gate (NOT-OR): This gate is an OR gate followed by a NOT gate. Its output is 1 only when all its inputs are 0.

c) XOR Gate (Exclusive OR): This gate has two inputs, and its output is 1 if and only if the inputs are different (one input is 1, and the other is 0).

d) XNOR Gate (Exclusive NOR): This gate is an XOR gate followed by a NOT gate. Its output is 1 if and only if both inputs are the same (either both 1 or both 0).

Symbols of Logic Gates

Each logic gate has a unique symbol to represent it in circuit diagrams. These symbols help to visualise the connections between different gates and the flow of signals within the circuit.

Creating Complex Circuits

We can create complex circuits that perform various functions by combining multiple logic gates. For example, we can design circuits for arithmetic operations, multiplexing, demultiplexing, memory storage, and more. The process typically involves designing a circuit using a combination of basic and derived gates, simplifying the circuit using Boolean algebra, and implementing the circuit using integrated circuits or other hardware components.

Example of a Complex Circuit

Let's consider designing a half-adder circuit, which adds two binary digits and produces a sum and a carry output. The half-adder can be created using an XOR gate for the sum output and an AND gate for the carry output. The inputs A and B are connected to both gates, with the XOR gate producing the sum (A $\oplus$ B) and the AND gate generating the carry (A $\cdot$ B).

COMBINATIONAL LOGIC CIRCUITS

Combinational logic circuits are digital circuits in which the output depends only on the current input values. In other words, the output is a combination of input signals processed through logic gates. Some common examples of combinational logic circuits include adders, subtracters, multiplexers, demultiplexers, and encoders. These circuits do not have memory elements, which means they do not store previous input states.

SEQUENTIAL LOGIC CIRCUITS

Sequential logic circuits are digital circuits where the output depends not only on the current input values but also on the history of the input signals. These circuits have memory elements, such as flip-flops and latches, that store previous input states. Sequential logic circuits can be classified into two types: synchronous and asynchronous. Synchronous sequential circuits use a clock signal to control the memory elements, while asynchronous sequential circuits do not rely on a clock signal. Examples of sequential logic circuits include counters, shift registers, and state machines.

FLIP-FLOPS AND LATCHES

Flip-flops and latches are fundamental memory elements in sequential logic circuits. They are capable of storing one bit of information (either a 0 or a 1).

a) Latches: A latch is a bistable device that can store one bit of data. It has two stable states, representing a 0 or a 1. The most common types of latches are the SR (set-reset) latch and the D (data) latch. An SR latch has two inputs, S (set) and R (reset), and two outputs, Q and its complement, Q'. When the S input is high, the Q output becomes 1, and when the R input is high, the Q output becomes 0. A D latch has a single data input and a clock input. When the clock input is high, the D latch stores the data from the input, and the output follows the data input.

b) Flip-Flops: A flip-flop is a more advanced form of a latch that is edge-triggered, meaning it only changes its output state when the clock signal transitions (either from 0 to 1 or 1 to 0). The most common types of flip-flops are the D flip-flop, the JK flip-flop, and the T (toggle) flip-flop. A D flip-flop is similar to a D latch, but it only updates its output when the clock signal transitions. A JK flip-flop has two inputs, J and K, and can be used as a versatile memory element. A T flip-flop has a single input and toggles its output state when the input is high.

By understanding these sub-topics, you will gain a deeper insight into the design and operation of digital circuits, even as a non-technical person.

CRYPTOGRAPHY AND ITS BASICS

Cryptography is the science and art of securing communication by transforming information into an unreadable format, ensuring that only authorised parties can access the data. It plays a crucial role in modern communication systems, especially in securing online transactions and protecting sensitive information. The main components of cryptography are encryption (converting plaintext into ciphertext) and decryption (converting ciphertext back to plaintext).

Cryptography is the science and art of securing communication by transforming information into an unreadable format, ensuring that only authorised parties can access the data. It plays a crucial role in modern communication systems, especially in securing online transactions and protecting sensitive information. The main components of cryptography are encryption (converting plaintext into ciphertext) and decryption (converting ciphertext back to plaintext).

HISTORY OF CRYPTOGRAPHY

The use of cryptography dates back thousands of years, with ancient civilisations such as the Egyptians and Greeks using simple substitution ciphers to protect their communications. Over time, more sophisticated methods were developed, like the Caesar cipher and the Vigènere cipher. In the 20th century, cryptography played a vital role in World War II, with the Enigma machine used by the Germans and the work of codebreakers like Alan Turing. Today, with the rise of computers and the internet, cryptography has become more complex, and numerous encryption algorithms and protocols have been developed to secure digital communication.

CRYPTOGRAPHIC PRIMITIVES

Cryptographic primitives are the fundamental building blocks of cryptographic systems. They consist of basic operations and algorithms that are used to construct more complex cryptographic protocols. Some common cryptographic primitives include hash functions, symmetric encryption algorithms (e.g., AES), asymmetric encryption algorithms (e.g., RSA), and digital signatures. These primitives are designed to provide essential security properties like confidentiality, integrity, authentication, and non-repudiation.

CRYPTANALYSIS AND ITS METHODS

Cryptanalysis is the process of analysing and breaking cryptographic systems to reveal the underlying plaintext or uncover the encryption key. Cryptanalysis aims not only to breach security systems but also to identify weaknesses in cryptographic algorithms and improve their security. Various methods are used in cryptanalysis, depending on the type of cipher and the available information. Some common cryptanalytic techniques include frequency analysis, brute-force attacks, and known-plaintext attacks.

CRYPTOGRAPHY STANDARDS AND PROTOCOLS

Cryptography standards and protocols are established guidelines and rules that govern the use of cryptographic algorithms and methods in various applications. These standards and protocols ensure the interoperability of systems and maintain a consistent level of security. Examples of cryptography standards include the Advanced Encryption Standard (AES) for symmetric encryption and the RSA algorithm for asymmetric encryption. Cryptographic protocols, like Secure Sockets Layer (SSL) and its successor Transport Layer Security (TLS), are used to secure communication over networks, ensuring the confidentiality and integrity of the transmitted data.

By understanding the basics of cryptography and its sub-topics, even non-technical people can appreciate the importance of secure communication and the various methods used to protect the information in the digital age.

Symmetric and Asymmetric Encryption

Encryption is a critical component of modern cryptography, ensuring the confidentiality of information by transforming plaintext data into an unreadable format (ciphertext). There are two primary types of encryption: symmetric and asymmetric. Understanding these concepts is essential for grasping the basics of securing digital communication.

Symmetric Encryption Algorithms (e.g., DES, AES):

Symmetric encryption uses a single key for both encryption and decryption. This means that the sender and receiver must share the same secret key to communicate securely. Two well-known symmetric encryption algorithms are the Data Encryption Standard (DES) and the Advanced Encryption Standard (AES). DES, developed in the 1970s, has since been replaced by AES due to its vulnerability to brute-force attacks. AES is currently the industry standard for symmetric encryption and is used worldwide to secure various forms of digital communication.

Stream Ciphers and Block Ciphers

Symmetric encryption algorithms can be further categorised into stream ciphers and block ciphers. Stream ciphers encrypt data one bit or byte at a time, making them suitable for applications with continuous data streams, such as audio and video streaming. Examples of stream ciphers include RC4 and Salsa20. Block ciphers, on the other hand, encrypt data in fixed-size blocks (e.g., 128 bits for AES). They are widely used in various applications, with examples including DES, AES, and Blowfish.

KEY MANAGEMENT AND DISTRIBUTION

A significant challenge with symmetric encryption is securely managing and distributing the shared secret key. If an attacker intercepts the key, they can decrypt the encrypted data. Key distribution methods include secure physical exchange, secure communication channels, and key distribution protocols like the Diffie-Hellman key exchange. Effective key management also requires proper storage, regular key rotation, and secure disposal of outdated keys.

ASYMMETRIC ENCRYPTION ALGORITHMS (E.G., RSA, ECC)

Asymmetric encryption, also known as public key cryptography, uses two separate keys: a public key for encryption and a private key for decryption. This eliminates the need for a shared secret key, as the public key can be freely distributed without compromising security. The RSA (Rivest-Shamir-Adleman) algorithm and the Elliptic Curve Cryptography (ECC) algorithm are two widely used asymmetric encryption algorithms. RSA is based on the mathematical properties of large prime numbers, while ECC relies on the mathematics of elliptic curves over finite fields. Both algorithms are commonly used for securing communication, digital signatures, and key exchange in various applications.

RSA ENCRYPTION ALGORITHM

RSA Encryption Algorithm is a public-key encryption algorithm widely used for secure data transmission over the internet. It was invented in 1977 by Ron Rivest, Adi Shamir, and Leonard Adleman and is named after their initials.

The algorithm works on the principle of prime factorisation. It uses two keys, a public key and a private key, to encrypt and decrypt data, respectively. The public key is known to everyone, while the private key is known only to the intended recipient.

The sender needs to know the recipient's public key to encrypt a message using RSA. The sender then performs certain mathematical operations on the message using the recipient's public key, which produces an encrypted message. This encrypted message can be safely transmitted over the internet to the recipient.

To decrypt the encrypted message, the recipient uses their private key, which is designed to undo the mathematical operations performed during encryption. The recipient then obtains the original message in plaintext.

The security of the RSA encryption algorithm is based on the difficulty of prime factorisation of large numbers. It is practically impossible to factorise large numbers, which makes RSA a secure encryption method.

RSA algorithm has several applications in modern computing, including secure protocols like HTTPS, secure email communication, and digital signatures.

RSA Encryption Algorithm is a widely used encryption algorithm in computer security. It encrypts data and messages sent over networks or stored in computer systems to ensure the information remains secure and private. Here are some examples of how RSA encryption can be used:

SECURE ONLINE TRANSACTIONS:

Online shopping is an example of how RSA encryption is used. When customers enter their credit card information, it is encrypted using RSA encryption before being transmitted over the internet. This ensures that hackers or other malicious actors cannot intercept the information.

EMAIL ENCRYPTION

Another example of RSA encryption is email encryption. By using RSA encryption, users can ensure that their emails are only accessible to the intended recipient. This is particularly useful when sending sensitive information such as financial information or confidential business information.

SECURE MESSAGING APPS

Messaging apps such as WhatsApp and Signal use RSA encryption to ensure that messages are secure and private. When a user sends a message, it is encrypted using RSA encryption before being transmitted over the internet. This ensures that hackers or other malicious actors cannot intercept the message.

PASSWORD PROTECTION

Password protection is another example of how RSA encryption is used. When a user creates a password, it is often encrypted using RSA encryption before being stored in a database. This ensures that if the database is hacked, the password cannot be easily decrypted and used to gain access to the user's account.

PUBLIC KEY INFRASTRUCTURE AND DIGITAL CERTIFICATES

Public Key Infrastructure (PKI) is pivotal in securing digital communication and transactions. It provides a framework for managing, distributing, and validating digital certificates, and verifying the identity of entities involved in digital communication. Let's examine PKI's essential components and concepts in a way accessible to non-technical individuals.

PUBLIC KEY INFRASTRUCTURE (PKI) AND ITS COMPONENTS

PKI provides a secure way to distribute, manage, and validate public keys for asymmetric encryption and digital signatures. PKI is a hierarchical system that comprises several components working together to establish trust and secure communication. The primary components of PKI include Certificate Authorities (CAs), Registration Authorities (RAs), digital certificates, and end entities (such as users, devices, or servers).

CERTIFICATE AUTHORITIES (CAs)

A Certificate Authority is a trusted third-party organisation responsible for issuing, renewing, and revoking digital certificates. CAs ensure that the digital certificates they issue are legitimate and can be trusted by other entities. The CA's public key is widely distributed and used to validate digital certificates issued by the CA. Some well-known CAs include Let's Encrypt, DigiCert, and GlobalSign.

DIGITAL CERTIFICATES AND THEIR FORMATS

A digital certificate is an electronic document that binds a public key to the identity of an individual, device, or organisation. It contains information such as the subject's name, the public key, the issuer's name, and the certificate's validity period. Digital certificates are used to verify the authenticity of a public key and its owner. The most common digital certificate format is X.509, which is a standard format used for various applications, such as Secure Sockets Layer (SSL) and Transport Layer Security (TLS) certificates for secure web browsing.

Figure 7 - This diagram simplifies the intricacies of how cryptography, including public key cryptography works.[7]

CERTIFICATE REVOCATION AND VALIDATION

Digital certificates have a finite validity period, after which they must be renewed. However, there are situations in which a certificate must be revoked before it expires, such as when a private key is compromised. To check the validity of a certificate, the revocation status is verified using mechanisms like Certificate Revocation Lists (CRLs) or the Online Certificate Status Protocol (OCSP). These tools help ensure that only valid certificates are used in secure communication.

Understanding PKI and digital certificates enables non-technical people to grasp the underlying concepts that facilitate trust and security in digital communication. By becoming familiar with the key components of PKI and their roles, anyone can better appreciate the importance of this infrastructure in today's digital landscape.

Machine Learning and Its Applications in Computing

Machine learning is a branch of artificial intelligence that enables computers to learn and improve from experience without being explicitly programmed. It has a wide range of applications in computing, from natural language processing to image recognition. Let's explore the different types of machine learning and some of their notable algorithms.

Supervised Learning and Its Algorithms

Supervised learning is a type of machine learning where the algorithm is trained on labelled data, meaning the input data has corresponding output values or "labels". The goal is for the algorithm to learn a relationship between the input and output, allowing it to make predictions on new, unseen data. Two common supervised learning tasks are regression and classification.

a. Regression: Regression algorithms predict continuous output values, such as predicting house prices based on various features. Examples of regression algorithms include linear regression and logistic regression.

b. Classification: Classification algorithms predict discrete output values, such as determining if an email is spam or not spam. Some popular classification algorithms are decision trees and random forests.

Unsupervised Learning and Its Algorithms

Unsupervised learning deals with unlabelled data, meaning the input data lacks corresponding output values. The goal is to uncover hidden patterns or structures within the data. Clustering and dimensionality reduction are two common unsupervised learning tasks.

a. Clustering: Clustering algorithms group data points with similar characteristics, such as grouping customers based on their purchasing habits. Examples of clustering algorithms are k-means and hierarchical clustering.

b. Dimensionality Reduction: Dimensionality reduction algorithms reduce the number of features in the dataset while preserving its essential structure. This is useful for visualising high-dimensional data or improving the efficiency of other machine learning algorithms. Principal Component Analysis (PCA) and t-distributed Stochastic Neighbour Embedding (t-SNE) are examples of dimensionality reduction techniques.

REINFORCEMENT LEARNING AND ITS APPLICATIONS

Reinforcement learning is a type of machine learning where an agent learns to make decisions by interacting with its environment. The agent receives rewards or penalties based on the actions it takes, helping it learn the best actions to achieve its goals. Applications of reinforcement learning include robotics, gaming, and self-driving cars.

DEEP LEARNING AND ITS NEURAL NETWORK ARCHITECTURES

Deep learning is a subset of machine learning that focuses on artificial neural networks with many layers, also known as deep neural networks. These networks are capable of learning complex patterns and representations from large amounts of data. Convolutional Neural Networks (CNNs) and Recurrent Neural Networks (RNNs) are two popular deep learning architectures.

a. Convolutional Neural Networks (CNNs): CNNs are designed for processing grid-like data, such as images. They are widely used in image recognition and computer vision tasks.

b. Recurrent Neural Networks (RNNs): RNNs are designed to process sequential data, such as time-series data or text. They are commonly used in natural languages processing tasks like language translation and sentiment analysis.

Machine learning has numerous applications in computing, making it an essential field for both technical and non-technical individuals to understand. By exploring its different types and algorithms, one can better appreciate the diverse range of problems machine learning can help solve.

Supervised and Unsupervised Learning Algorithms

In machine learning, two primary approaches are supervised and unsupervised. These methods allow computers to learn patterns and make predictions based on input data. Let's explore some popular algorithms for each of these approaches.

Regression Algorithms

Regression algorithms are supervised learning techniques that predict continuous output values. They are widely used in various applications, such as predicting sales figures, stock prices, or house prices.

a. Linear Regression: Linear regression is a straightforward algorithm that predicts output values based on a linear relationship between input features and output values. It aims to find the best-fitting straight line that minimises the difference between actual and predicted values.

*b. **Logistic Regression:*** Logistic regression is similar to linear regression but is used for predicting binary outcomes. It models the probability of an event, such as determining if a customer will make a purchase.

Classification Algorithms

Classification algorithms are another type of supervised learning technique that predicts discrete output values. They are used in various applications, such as spam detection, image classification, or medical diagnosis.

*a. **Decision Trees:*** Decision trees are a popular classification algorithm that recursively splits input data into subsets based on the values of input features. The tree is built by selecting the best feature at each node to maximise information gain.

b. Random Forests: Random forests are an extension of decision trees that build multiple trees and aggregate their predictions. This ensemble technique improves accuracy and reduces the risk of overfitting.

CLUSTERING ALGORITHMS

Clustering algorithms are a type of unsupervised learning technique that groups data points with similar characteristics. They are used in customer segmentation, anomaly detection, or image segmentation applications.

a. K-means: K-means is a popular clustering algorithm that partitions the data into a predetermined number of clusters (k). It iteratively assigns data points to the nearest cluster centre and updates the centre's position until convergence.

b. Hierarchical Clustering: Hierarchical clustering is another clustering technique that builds a tree-like structure of nested clusters. It can be performed using either a bottom-up (agglomerative) or top-down (divisive) approach.

DIMENSIONALITY REDUCTION ALGORITHMS

Dimensionality reduction algorithms are unsupervised learning techniques that reduce the number of features in the dataset while preserving its essential structure. They are useful for visualisation, improving the efficiency of other machine learning algorithms, or removing noise.

a. Principal Component Analysis (PCA): PCA is a widely used dimensionality reduction technique that projects the data onto a lower-dimensional space. It identifies the directions with the highest variance and uses them to create new features.

b. t-distributed Stochastic Neighbour Embedding (t-SNE): t-SNE is a more advanced dimensionality reduction technique that maps high-dimensional data into a lower-dimensional space while preserving the relative distances between data points. It is particularly useful for visualising complex data structures.

Understanding supervised and unsupervised learning algorithms is crucial for CSE students, as they form the foundation of many real-world applications. By exploring these algorithms, students can gain insights into various techniques and their practical use in solving problems.

Neural Networks and Deep Learning

Neural networks and deep learning are advanced techniques in machine learning that have gained significant attention due to their impressive performance in a wide range of applications. These methods are inspired by the structure and function of the human brain and are capable of learning complex patterns and representations.

Feedforward Neural Networks

Feedforward neural networks are the most basic type of artificial neural network. They consist of multiple layers of interconnected nodes or neurons, including an input layer, one or more hidden layers, and an output layer. Information flows from the input layer through the hidden layers to the output layer in a forward direction without any feedback loops. The architecture of these networks can vary in terms of the number of hidden layers and neurons in each layer.

Convolutional Neural Networks (CNNs)

Convolutional neural networks (CNNs) are a specialised type of neural network designed to process grid-like data, such as images or time-series data. CNNs utilise convolutional layers, which automatically learn local features from the input data, reducing the need for manual feature engineering. These networks are particularly effective in image recognition tasks, such as object detection, facial recognition, and image classification.

Recurrent Neural Networks (RNNs)

Recurrent neural networks (RNNs) are another type of neural network that can process sequential data, such as time-series data or text. RNNs have connections between neurons that form directed cycles, allowing them to maintain a hidden state that can capture information from previous time steps. This architecture makes RNNs particularly suitable for natural language processing tasks, such as language translation, text generation, and sentiment analysis.

DEEP LEARNING FRAMEWORKS

Deep learning frameworks are software libraries that provide tools and abstractions for building, training, and deploying neural networks. Some popular deep learning frameworks include TensorFlow, PyTorch, and Keras. These frameworks offer various features, such as:

a. Pre-built layers and models: Deep learning frameworks provide pre-built layers (e.g., convolutional, recurrent, or fully connected layers) and models (e.g., pre-trained neural networks) that simplify the process of building custom architectures.

b. Automatic differentiation: These frameworks handle the computation of gradients through automatic differentiation, simplifying the implementation of backpropagation and optimising neural networks.

c. GPU acceleration: Deep learning frameworks are designed to take advantage of Graphics Processing Units (GPUs) for faster training and inference, enabling researchers and developers to work with larger datasets and more complex models.

d. Visualisation and debugging tools: Many deep learning frameworks come with tools for visualising and debugging the training process, which can help understand and improve the performance of neural networks.

Understanding neural networks and deep learning is essential for CSE students, as these techniques have revolutionised various fields, such as computer vision, natural language processing, and speech recognition. By exploring these topics, students can gain valuable insights into state-of-the-art techniques and their applications in solving complex problems.

Chapter 6 Exercises and More

Below you will find a set of practice questions and their corresponding answers. In addition, this section includes key takeaways and symbols from the chapter to help reinforce your understanding of the material.

Practice Questions

1. Explain the concept of Boolean algebra and its importance in digital logic circuits. How do Boolean operators affect the outcome of a logic operation?
2. What are De Morgan's laws, and how can they be used to simplify Boolean expressions?
3. Describe the basic logic gates (AND, OR, NOT) and their symbols. How can these gates be combined to create more complex circuits?
4. Explain the difference between symmetric and asymmetric encryption. Provide examples of popular algorithms used for each type of encryption.
5. What is the role of public key infrastructure (PKI) in securing digital communications? Describe the key components of a PKI system.
6. What is a digital certificate, and how is it used in securing online communications? Explain the process of certificate validation and revocation.
7. Describe supervised learning and unsupervised learning, and provide examples of common algorithms used in each category.
8. What are the key differences between feedforward neural networks, convolutional neural networks (CNNs), and recurrent neural networks (RNNs)? Provide examples of the types of problems each architecture is best suited for.

9. Explain the concept of dimensionality reduction, and discuss how PCA (principal component analysis) and t-SNE (t-distributed stochastic neighbour embedding) can be used to reduce the number of features in a dataset.
10. Discuss the importance of deep learning frameworks, such as TensorFlow and PyTorch, in the development of neural network models. Describe some of the key features provided by these frameworks to simplify the process of building and training neural networks.

KEY TAKEAWAYS FROM THIS CHAPTER

- Boolean algebra is a branch of mathematics that deals with binary values (0 and 1) and is used extensively in digital logic circuits, which form the basis of computing systems.
- Basic logic gates, including AND, OR, and NOT, can be combined to create complex circuits such as combinational and sequential logic circuits.
- De Morgan's laws provide a powerful tool for simplifying Boolean expressions, thus allowing for more efficient circuit designs.
- Cryptography is the science of securing information through various encryption and decryption techniques, with a rich history dating back to ancient civilisations.
- Symmetric and asymmetric encryption are the two main types of encryption algorithms. Symmetric algorithms use the same key for encryption and decryption, and asymmetric algorithms use different keys (public and private).
- Public Key Infrastructure (PKI) and digital certificates are essential components in secure communication, providing a framework for establishing trust among parties.
- Machine learning is a subset of artificial intelligence that enables computers to learn from data without explicit programming and includes supervised, unsupervised, and reinforcement learning.

- Supervised and unsupervised learning algorithms cover a wide range of techniques, such as regression, classification, clustering, and dimensionality reduction, to address various data analysis tasks.
- Neural networks and deep learning are advanced machine learning techniques that leverage complex architectures and multiple layers to capture intricate patterns and features in data, with applications in image recognition, natural language processing, and more.
- Various deep learning frameworks, such as TensorFlow and PyTorch, are available to help developers efficiently implement and train neural network models, speeding up the development process and facilitating experimentation.

SYMBOLS AND NOTIONS

Boolean operators:
∧ (AND)
∨ (OR)
¬ (NOT)

Logic gates:
AND gate: & or ·
OR gate: ≥1 or +
NOT gate: ¬ or '

De Morgan's laws:
(A ∧ B)' = A' ∨ B'
(A ∨ B)' = A' ∧ B'

Cryptography:
Symmetric key: Ks
Public key: Kpub
Private key: Kpriv

Plaintext: P
Ciphertext: C
Encryption function: E
Decryption function: D

Machine learning:
Learning rate: α (alpha)
Weights: w
Bias: b
Loss function: L
Error rate: ε (epsilon)

Neural networks:
Activation function: σ (sigma)
Input layer: X
Hidden layer: H
Output layer: Y
Convolutional layer: C
Pooling layer: P
Recurrent layer: R

These symbols and notations have been used throughout the chapter to explain various concepts and their applications.

FURTHER STUDIES AND RESOURCES

Khan Academy - Introduction to Digital Logic: This resource offers a beginner-friendly introduction to digital logic, covering topics such as Boolean algebra, logic gates, and combinational circuits.
https://www.khanacademy.org/computing/computer-science/computing-systems#intro-to-digital-logic

Coursera - Cryptography I by Stanford University: This online course provides a comprehensive introduction to cryptography, covering topics

such as symmetric and asymmetric encryption, cryptographic primitives, and cryptanalysis.
https://www.coursera.org/learn/crypto

Machine Learning Mastery - A Gentle Introduction to Machine Learning: This blog post provides a concise introduction to machine learning, covering supervised, unsupervised, and reinforcement learning, as well as common algorithms and their applications.
https://machinelearningmastery.com/a-gentle-introduction-to-machine-learning/

DeepLearning.ai - Neural Networks and Deep Learning: This online course is part of the Deep Learning Specialisation on Coursera and covers neural networks, deep learning, and their applications, including convolutional neural networks (CNNs) and recurrent neural networks (RNNs).
https://www.coursera.org/learn/neural-networks-deep-learning

TensorFlow - Get Started with TensorFlow: TensorFlow is a popular open-source deep learning framework developed by Google. This official guide provides a step-by-step introduction to using TensorFlow for various machine learning tasks, including tutorials and example projects.
https://www.tensorflow.org/overview

ANSWERS TO THE PRACTICE QUESTIONS

1. Boolean algebra is a branch of mathematics that deals with binary variables (0 and 1) and logical operations. It is essential in digital logic circuits because it provides a way to represent and manipulate logical expressions, which form the basis of digital computing. Boolean operators, such as AND, OR, and NOT, determine the outcome of a logic operation based on the input values according to their respective truth tables.
2. De Morgan's laws are two transformation rules that can be used to simplify Boolean expressions. They state that negating an AND

operation is equivalent to the OR operation of the negated inputs, and vice versa. Mathematically, they can be expressed as:
- $\neg(A \land B) = \neg A \lor \neg B$
- $\neg(A \lor B) = \neg A \land \neg B$
- These laws help to convert complex expressions into simpler ones, which can be useful in designing and simplifying digital circuits.

3. The basic logic gates are fundamental building blocks of digital circuits. These gates can be combined to create more complex circuits, such as half-adders, full-adders, and multiplexers, which perform more advanced functions. The AND gate outputs 1 only if both inputs are 1, the OR gate outputs 1 if either input is 1, and the NOT gate inverts its input.

4. Symmetric encryption uses the same key for encryption and decryption, whereas asymmetric encryption uses a pair of keys (public and private). Popular symmetric encryption algorithms include Data Encryption Standard (DES) and Advanced Encryption Standard (AES), while popular asymmetric encryption algorithms include RSA and Elliptic Curve Cryptography (ECC).

5. Public Key Infrastructure (PKI) is a system that provides secure digital communication through the use of cryptographic techniques. Key components of a PKI system include certificate authorities (CAs), which issue digital certificates, and registration authorities (RAs), which authenticate the entities requesting certificates.

6. A digital certificate is an electronic document that uses a digital signature to bind a public key to an entity's identity. It is used in securing online communications by verifying the sender's authenticity and encrypting data. Certificate validation involves checking that a trusted CA issues the certificate, which has not expired or been revoked. Certificate revocation occurs when a certificate is no longer considered valid due to a key compromise or change in the certificate holder's information.

7. Supervised learning involves training a model with labelled data, where the input-output relationship is known. Common supervised learning algorithms include linear regression, logistic regression, decision trees, and random forests. On the other hand, unsupervised learning involves training a model without labelled data, and discovering patterns or structures within the data. Common unsupervised learning algorithms include k-means clustering, hierarchical clustering, PCA, and t-SNE.

8. Feedforward neural networks are basic neural networks with no cycles, where information flows in one direction from input to output. Recurrent neural networks (RNNs) have cycles that allow them to maintain a hidden state, making them suitable for sequence-based problems like natural language processing. Convolutional neural networks (CNNs) are designed for image recognition and use convolutional layers to learn spatial features.

9. Dimensionality reduction is reducing the number of features in a dataset, which can improve computational efficiency and reduce noise. Principal component analysis (PCA) is a linear technique that projects data onto a lower-dimensional space while preserving the maximum amount of variance. T-distributed stochastic neighbour embedding (t-SNE) is a non-linear technique that aims to preserve the local structure of the data by minimizing the divergence between probability distributions in the original and lower-dimensional spaces.

10. Deep learning frameworks like TensorFlow and PyTorch simplify the process of building and training deep learning models by providing pre-built layers, optimisers, and other necessary components. These frameworks also offer GPU support for accelerated training and a rich ecosystem of tools and libraries that can be used for various applications such as computer vision, natural language processing, and reinforcement learning. TensorFlow is developed by Google, while PyTorch is developed

by Facebook's AI Research lab. Both frameworks have extensive documentation, community support, and are widely used in academia and industry.

INDEX

- Agile Methodology: An iterative and incremental approach to software development that emphasises flexibility, collaboration, and customer satisfaction.
- Agile Project Management: An approach to project management that emphasises flexibility, collaboration, and continuous improvement, often used in software development projects.
- Artificial Intelligence (AI): The simulation of human intelligence processes by machines, including tasks such as visual perception, speech recognition, decision-making, and language translation.
- BIOS (Basic Input/Output System): Firmware used to initialise and test hardware components during the boot process of a computer.
- Central Processing Unit (CPU) - The CPU is the "brain" of the computer that performs calculations and controls the flow of information.
- CLI: A Command-Line Interface (CLI) is a user interface requiring users to enter text commands to interact with a computer system—Graphical User Interface (GUI) vs Command-Line Interface (CLI).
- Cloud Computing: Cloud computing delivers computing services, such as servers, storage, databases, and software, over the internet. It allows users to access these services on-demand without needing on-site infrastructure.
- Cloud-Native Computing: An approach to software development that utilises cloud computing infrastructure and services to build and deploy scalable and resilient applications.
- Code Editors: Software applications designed specifically for editing and writing code, providing features such as syntax highlighting, code completion, and code navigation.

- Computer Hardware: Computer hardware refers to the physical components of a computer, such as a motherboard, CPU, RAM, storage devices, and input/output devices.
- Computer Networks: A computer network is a collection of computers and other devices that are connected together to share resources and communicate with each other.
- Computer System: A computer system is a combination of hardware and software that works together to perform computing tasks.
- Continuous Integration and Continuous Delivery (CI/CD): A set of practices that involve automating the building, testing, and deployment of software to increase efficiency, reduce errors, and improve the speed of software delivery.
- CPU: The Central Processing Unit (CPU) is the computer's brain that performs most of the processing of instructions.
- Cybersecurity: The practice of protecting computer systems, networks, and sensitive information from unauthorised access, theft, or damage.
- Data Science: A field that combines statistical and computational methods to extract insights and knowledge from data, often used in applications such as predictive modelling, pattern recognition, and data visualisation.
- Debuggers: Software tools used by developers to identify and fix errors, defects, and other issues in software systems.
- DevOps: An approach that emphasises collaboration and communication between development and operations teams, aiming to streamline the software development lifecycle and improve the speed and reliability of software delivery.
- DNS (Domain Name System): A system that translates domain names (such as www.google.com) into IP addresses that computers can use to communicate over a network.
- Edge Computing: Edge computing is a distributed computing paradigm that brings computation and data storage closer to the

- location where it is needed to improve response time and save bandwidth.
- Ethernet is a wired networking technology that uses cables to connect devices to a network.
- Ethernet Port: An Ethernet port is a connector on a computer that is used to connect to a wired network. Its function is to send and receive data between the computer and other devices on the network.
- File System - A method operating systems use to organise and store files and directories on a storage device.
- FPGA (Field-Programmable Gate Array): An integrated circuit that can be programmed and reprogrammed after manufacturing to perform specific logic functions.
- FTP (File Transfer Protocol): A protocol used for transferring files between computers over a network.
- Graphical User Interface (GUI) - An interface that allows users to interact with a computer using graphical elements, such as icons and menus.
- GUI: A Graphical User Interface (GUI) is a user interface that allows users to interact with a computer system using visual elements such as icons, buttons, and menus.
- Hard Disk Drive (HDD) - A type of storage device that uses spinning disks to store and retrieve data.
- HCI (Human-Computer Interaction): The study of how humans interact with computers and how to design computer systems that are easy to use and intuitive for humans.
- History of Software Engineering: An overview of the evolution of software engineering as a discipline from its early beginnings to modern software development practices.
- Integrated Development Environment (IDE): A software application that provides comprehensive tools and features for developing software, including code editors, debuggers, compilers, and build tools.

- Interaction: Interaction refers to how users interact with a computer system, including the user interface, input devices, and output devices.
- Introduction to Software Engineering: A discipline concerned with the systematic approach to software development, operation, and maintenance.
- IoT (Internet of Things): A network of interconnected devices that are able to collect and exchange data through the internet.
- IP (Internet Protocol): A protocol used for routing data packets between devices on a network, including the internet.
- IP Address - A unique identifier assigned to each device on a network, allowing them to communicate with each other using the Internet Protocol.
- Kanban Methodology: A visual workflow management approach that emphasises continuous delivery and improvement, flexibility, and collaboration.
- Lean Methodology: A management philosophy and approach to software development that focuses on minimising waste, optimising resources, and maximising value for the customer.
- Local Area Network (LAN) - A network that covers a small area, such as a home, office, or school.
- Machine Learning: A subfield of AI that enables machines to learn from data and make predictions or decisions based on that learning.
- Microservices: An architectural approach to software development that involves breaking down applications into smaller, independent services that can be developed, deployed, and scaled separately.
- Motherboard - The motherboard is the main circuit board in a computer that connects all the components together.
- NTFS (New Technology File System): A file system used by modern versions of the Windows operating system that provides advanced features such as file compression, encryption, and permissions.

- Operating System (OS) - The software that manages the computer hardware and software resources and provides common services for computer programs.
- PaaS (Platform as a Service): A cloud computing service model in which a provider offers a platform for users to develop, run, and manage applications.
- Protocol: A protocol is a set of rules and standards that dictate how devices on a network communicate with each other.
- Random Access Memory (RAM) - RAM is a volatile memory that temporarily stores data that the CPU is currently working on.
- Read-Only Memory (ROM) - ROM is a type of non-volatile memory that stores data that cannot be modified.
- ROM: Read-Only Memory (ROM) is a type of non-volatile memory that stores data that cannot be modified.
- Router - A networking device connecting multiple networks and directing data traffic between them.
- SaaS (Software as a Service): A cloud computing service model in which a provider offers access to software applications hosted on their servers and accessed over the internet.
- Scrum Methodology: A framework for agile software development that emphasises teamwork, communication, and iterative progress towards a well-defined goal.
- Serverless Architecture: An architectural approach that allows developers to build and run applications without managing servers or infrastructure by utilising cloud computing services and event-driven programming models.
- Serverless Computing - A model of cloud computing where the cloud provider manages the infrastructure and automatically allocates resources as needed.
- SMTP (Simple Mail Transfer Protocol): A protocol for sending email messages between computers over a network.
- Software Configuration Management: The process of identifying, organising, and controlling changes to software products

and related artefacts throughout the software development life cycle.
- Software Design: The process of creating a detailed plan or blueprint for a software system that defines its architecture, components, interfaces, and data.
- Software Development Life Cycle (SDLC): The process of developing software, from the initial planning stage through maintenance and support.
- Software Development Methodologies: The various approaches to developing software systems, each with its own set of principles, practices, and techniques.
- Software Development Tools: The various software tools used by software developers to design, code, test, debug, and maintain software systems.
- Software Engineering Ethics: A field of study that addresses the ethical considerations and responsibilities of software developers and engineers, including privacy, security, and the impact of technology on society.
- Software Maintenance: The process of modifying, updating, or otherwise changing existing software to correct errors, improve performance, or enhance functionality.
- Software Metrics and Measurement: The process of quantifying and evaluating various aspects of software products, processes, and resources to improve software quality, productivity, and efficiency.
- Software Project Management: The discipline of planning, organising, and managing resources to successfully complete software projects on time, within budget, and to specified quality standards.
- Software Quality Assurance (SQA): The process of ensuring that software products and processes meet the specified requirements and quality standards.

- Software Requirements: The process of identifying, analysing, documenting, and validating the needs and constraints of stakeholders for a software system.
- Software Testing: The process of evaluating a software system or component to determine whether it meets the specified requirements and quality standards.
- Solid-State Drive (SSD) - A type of storage device that uses flash memory to store and retrieve data.
- TCP (Transmission Control Protocol): A protocol used for transmitting data over a network in a reliable and ordered manner.
- Testing Frameworks: Software tools and libraries used by developers to automate and manage software testing processes and tasks.
- TLS (Transport Layer Security): A security protocol that provides secure communication over a network, often used for secure web browsing and email.
- UDP (User Datagram Protocol): A protocol used for transmitting data over a network in a fast and unreliable manner.
- UEFI (Unified Extensible Firmware Interface): A newer type of firmware used to initialise and test hardware components during the boot process of a computer, replacing the older BIOS system.
- Usability: Usability is the degree to which specified users can use a system to achieve specified goals with effectiveness, efficiency, and satisfaction in a specified context.
- User-Centred Design: A design approach that involves understanding the needs and goals of users and incorporating their feedback throughout the design process to create products and services that are easy to use and meet their needs.
- UX (User Experience): The overall experience that a user has when interacting with a computer system or application, encompassing factors such as ease of use, efficiency, and satisfaction.

- Version Control Systems (VCS): Software tools and practices for managing changes to source code and other software artefacts, enabling collaboration and version control.
- Virtualisation: Virtualisation is creating a virtual version of a computing resource, such as a server, operating system, or network. It is used to run multiple virtual machines on a single physical machine.
- VPN (Virtual Private Network): A network connection that provides a secure, private connection over a public network such as the internet.
- WAN (Wide Area Network): A network of connected devices that are located in a large geographic area, such as a country or the entire world.
- Waterfall Methodology: A linear, sequential approach to software development that divides the development process into distinct phases, each of which must be completed before proceeding to the next.

TABLE OF FIGURES

Figure 1 - Graphs such as these are among the objects studied by discrete mathematics 7
Figure 2 - A set of polygons in an Euler diagram 13
Figure 3 - Visualising functions 19
Figure 4 - A directed graph represented by an adjacency matrix 23
Figure 5 - A schematic diagram used in logic theory to depict collections of sets and represent their relationships 46
Figure 6 - An example of the bipartite graph-partitioning-based approach for task decomposition on two processors 56
Figure 7 - This diagram simplifies the intricacies of how cryptography, including public key cryptography works. 174

OTHER BOOKS IN THIS SERIES

This book is part of a series of books written on Computer Science Engineering (CSE) for the non-CSE Enthusiasts' initiative by Enamul Haque.

Book – 1	Book – 2	Book – 3
Introduction to Computer Systems and Software Engineering	Introduction to Mathematics for Computing (Algorithms and Data Structures)	Introduction to Digital literacy and the future of computing

ISBN:	ISBN:	ISBN:
9781447790563	9781447771302	9781445273921

Available: at https://www.lulu.com/spotlight/authorenam

ABOUT THE AUTHOR

Enamul Haque (এনামুল হক) is an industry veteran and thought leader with almost 30 years of experience in the IT industry. Throughout his career, Enamul has worked with some of the world's most reputable companies, including Wipro, Microsoft, Capgemini, Nokia, and HCL Technologies, as well as international organisations like the United Nations High Commissioner for Refugees (UNHCR) and International Telecommunication Union (ITU).

As a data whisperer, Enamul is renowned for his expertise in AI-driven RPA (Intelligent Process Automation), service integration and management, and digital transformation. He has helped several Fortune 500 businesses navigate the rapidly changing technology landscape and capitalise on its opportunities.

Enamul is also an accomplished author and researcher who has written on many topics, including IT Service Management, Cloud Computing, AI, IoT, and Big Data analytics. His deep understanding of the industry and ability to stay at the forefront of technological advancements have made him a sought-after speaker and guest lecturer at the University of Coventry's London campus.

Enamul holds a licence en science Informatique from the University of Geneva, a degree in mathematics and analytics from the Swiss Federal Institute of Technology (EPFL), Lausanne, and a degree in machine learning and AI from the University of Helsinki. He recently received a leadership and mentoring certification from Harvard Business School.

Enamul's vast and diverse experience, combined with his passion for technology and its impact on the world, makes him a true thought leader in the industry. He stays at the forefront of emerging trends and is dedicated to helping organisations embrace digital transformation and thrive in today's ever-evolving technology landscape.

Enamul has been at the forefront of some of the most significant technological advancements of the past three decades, including the rise of cloud computing, artificial intelligence, and the Internet of Things. Throughout his career, he has consistently demonstrated his ability to anticipate trends and identify opportunities for innovation. Enamul's expertise in service integration and management has been precious in helping organisations navigate the complex landscape of emerging technologies and ensure they stay ahead of the curve. His passion for lifelong learning has kept him on the cutting edge of IT innovation, and he is always excited to share his insights with others.

In addition to his work in the IT industry, Enamul is an accomplished author and researcher. He has published numerous articles on topics ranging from IT service management to cloud computing to big data analytics. He is a sought-after speaker and has presented at conferences and seminars worldwide. Enamul's ability to explain complex technical concepts in accessible language has made him a valuable resource for businesses looking to stay up-to-date with the latest developments in the IT field.

Enamul is also committed to giving back to his community. Whether mentoring young professionals, volunteering with local charities, or leading tech initiatives in developing countries, Enamul is dedicated to making a difference in the world. He has volunteered with several non-profit organisations over the years and is passionate about using technology to positively impact society. He believes that the IT industry is responsible for promoting social good, and he always looks for ways to use his expertise to help those in need.

Get all my books from here: https://www.lulu.com/spotlight/authorenam

NOTES AND REFERENCES

[1] Cover picture by: Ricardo Lima: Photo by Ricardo Lima: https://www.pexels.com/photo/close-up-of-parrot-15311317/

[2] Discrete mathematics: https://en.wikipedia.org/wiki/Discrete_mathematics

[3] By PolygonsSet.svg: kismalac / derivative work: Stephan Kulla (Stephan Kulla) - PolygonsSet.svg, CC0, https://commons.wikimedia.org/w/index.php?curid=39323364

[4] By User:Banerjee - Own work, CC BY-SA 2.5, https://en.wikiversity.org/w/index.php?curid=39433

[5] Massive Parallelism With Gpus for Centrality Ranking in Complex Networks: https://www.researchgate.net/publication/274143903_Massive_Parallelism_With_Gpus_for_Centrality_Ranking_in_Complex_Networks

[6] Venn Diagram - https://mathworld.wolfram.com/VennDiagram.html

[7] The Complete Guide to Public Key Cryptography: https://history-computer.com/public-key-cryptography-complete-guide/

www.ingramcontent.com/pod-product-compliance
Lightning Source LLC
Chambersburg PA
CBHW071418170526
45165CB00001B/318